"When I met Ann, she gave off an aura of selflessness and a genuine person of goodwill. In a group of people, she stands out as a gentle person with a pleasant, inviting smile. Individually, however, she is as strong as one could be, and she is also very intelligent. Perhaps one of her strongest characteristics is that she is comfortable with herself, whether walking in the woods, hiking, or speaking to a large audience. She is special, and it has been wonderful working and learning from her. I can't think of another person in my years who is so comfortable with herself and at the same time draws one to her like a magnet. Ann has much more time to influence others, and the aura that surrounds her will always be remembered."

—Jimmy Bailey
Commercial and Investment Real Estate Business, SC House of
Representatives, Owner, Non-Profit, YEScarolina

"I first met Ann at a wellness seminar where she was the presenter. I was eager to learn about this Isotonic Nutrition. Her knowledge of nutrition and her passion for helping others to achieve ultimate health was very impressive. After my success with the vitamins, Ann came to my house, held several seminars, and shared her knowledge with many of my friends. Ann's individual consultation helped each person to achieve a healthier lifestyle. Ann is a very successful business owner and has the same passion for helping others to learn and achieve their success as business owners. She has always been patient and generous with her time, never hesitating to go out of her way to make the right things happen. Through the years, Ann has unselfishly guided me with nutrition and business management tips. I would recommend Ann to anyone looking for a business partner, nutritionist, or friend."

—Dianne Larsen
Retired Teacher

"I have known Ann since I was a young child but have worked with her professionally for twenty years. I have worked with Ann, learning to implement NutraMetrix business systems and nutraceuticals into my practices. We have helped individuals reach optimal health by utilizing nutraceuticals and providing an educational system for them. We have also worked together, assisting people with DNA-mapping results to provide an optimal health regimen for them very specific to their health needs. Ann has assisted me in my knowledge of nutrition and has been a huge encouragement to me to learn more. She is always available to answer any questions I have. I would highly recommend individuals who are looking to optimize their health or health professionals looking for another income source to expand their business to work with Ann."

—Colleen Oliver
Branches of the Vine, LLC,
Physical Therapist in Private Practice for Over Thirty Years

"Ann Riedy is an amazing person. I am so glad she came into my life in 2004. Ann challenged my thought processes about dreaming again and finding a way to be able to fuel those dreams. I had fallen into the rut of getting a good education, a good job, and starting a family, and I had my head down, working really hard at all of it. Ann walked into my life and said, 'What is it that you wanted to do when you graduated from high school?' 'What did you dream about?' Ann showed me the way through a systematic approach of a business that I could do part-time. I'm truly grateful for her persistence, commitment, and discipline in training me. With the truth and strength of her character, I learned to become an online entrepreneur. Ann's honesty, caring nature, and straightforward approach are a blessing to those interested in self-improvement."

—Pam Torgerson
Retired College Professor,
Million Dollar Club Earner, Health with Pam, Inc.

"Ann is a very dedicated person. I have taken two different classes from her. She explains things, so it is easy to understand. Everyone who took her classes improved in the areas they were seeking. I gained confidence after taking Ann's personal training class, and with her help, I was able to teach my own classes and pay it forward. Ann builds up your confidence and encourages you. She walks/talks with you until you are able to do it alone. Then, she is still there to answer questions and help if needed. Ann always wants to learn. She shares her wealth of information in a way that is interesting and leaves you wanting to know more. Ann deeply cares for people and wants to help them improve their lives."

—Pamela Kopp
Volunteer at a Horse Ranch (Teaching Children),
Church Office Work

"To know Ann is a true honor. She has been a fantastic mentor and anchor, helping me on my health journey since 2008. Ann is a blessing to be around. She cares deeply about people and is always willing to give a helping hand on their personal health journeys. Ann is very determined to keep going no matter what. She's always moving forward, continuing with her education, teaching others, and sharing her knowledge. She keeps everyone encouraged and moving forward. Part of Ann's gift is seeing the best in people and bringing that out, truly helping them see they are worth it. She spends her time helping others become the best they can be and honor themselves. I am grateful and thankful that God brought Ann into our lives."

—Sonya Swan
Mom, Ranch Wife, Entrepreneur

IMPACT
LEADERSHIP

WITH ANN RIEDY

ALSO FEATURING
OTHER TOP AUTHORS

Table of Contents

CHAPTER 1

BEING ENOUGH

By Ann Riedy

Ever meet a person who everyone seems to love? The funny one, fun to be around, and a people magnet—always laughing or making others laugh. I always liked to be around a person like that because they made me feel like I was a part of something that I could never experience by myself.

I've always called myself shy. I was the shadow. I was someone who needed to be by someone's side and didn't like to be left to my own devices as I couldn't find anything to say. So, I became the shadow.

I can't say I liked it. I've always wanted to be like everybody else, and I wondered, 'What is wrong with me?' I never felt like I was enough. I didn't understand myself or why I was the way I was—living in the shadow but not enjoying myself along the journey. The struggle was real, and the harsh judgment towards self was constant.

One day, I heard someone say that you become what you think about all day long. I wondered what the heck that meant because my thoughts were not too kind to me. I started the process of really analyzing what and why my thoughts kept me busy all day long, and I wanted to find out what I could do to change it.

One day I realized something important: "I am Enough!"

"I am Enough!" Have you ever said that yourself? I hope you have, and I hope you do every single day because it is the truth.

YOU ARE ENOUGH! YOU ARE AWESOME! YOU ARE BEAUTIFUL! YOU ARE AMAZING! YOU ARE SO BRAVE!

Although, chances are that if you are like me, you haven't said those words. But if you said those words as a small child, you might have been made to feel like it was wrong or that you were being conceited and full of yourself. After all, that is not something we wanted to be.

Last year, I had some time on my hands during the pandemic, and I joined a couple of coaching classes. One of the sessions opened my eyes to a whole lot of stuff, one of which is this lie we tell ourselves: we are *not* enough.

It sounds something like this:

I don't know enough. I don't look good enough. My voice isn't good enough. I'm not tall, thin, cute, young, clever, or whatever enough. I'm just not good enough. I didn't say enough. I didn't do enough. I should have . . . I shouldn't have . . .

You get the drift.

I learned about something called our inner critic and how it always looks for something to keep us down, stop us from moving forward, and hold us still. One of the classes talked about something that really spoke to me: *The Vow to Be Invisible.* Wow! That spoke to me because it was how I felt about putting myself out there in the world to offer my help to people because of all the reasons stated above: the whole 'I'm not enough' saga and the inner critic taking over and keeping me silent.

Once I had a name for all this "stuff" going on in my head, I could finally take action because, before that, I had no idea what made me so different. I hadn't the slightest clue of what made me stay silent and not move forward to achieve my greatness, goals, and my own unique ability to connect with people.

One time, a coach from one of the classes I attended asked me a few questions about my goals and passions in life. I had a hard time answering her. But I *did* know that if others could do it, so could I.

You see, I love to learn, study, and share the information I'm learning with anyone who needs it. And when I revealed to someone all the books I'd read and all the "binders" of notes from classes I'd taken, I was told,

"Ann, you know enough!"

"You know enough to fill many lifetimes of helping people!"

"You just need to 'feel' like you *are* enough, and everything will change in your life."

Really??? Well, how do you go about all of this?

I'm going to share with you the three most important steps that I took to help me overcome these inner critical voices and step into my greatness. I will show you how you can confidently, and without reserve, say to yourself boldly, "I AM ENOUGH! I AM AWESOME! I AM BEAUTIFUL, I AM AMAZING, and I AM SO BRAVE!"

I'm sure you've heard the saying, 'You become what you think about all day long' or 'You become what you say to yourself.' Other variations include 'what you are listening to' and 'what you hear every day.'

If the above is true, we really need to examine what that means, and more importantly, what it is that we hear every day that affects our lives and makes us who we are.

So, let's dive into the three steps you can take to begin the process of leaning into the true, wonderful feeling of *I Am Enough!*

Step One

The first part of the first step is to be aware of and examine your self-talk. Are you kind or critical of yourself? More importantly, what desires and beliefs lie deep inside of you? Who is your private self, your invisible self, that you don't let anyone see? You know that quiet little space inside of you that no one can get to, that no one can ruin. It's a secret. Do you see that person inside of you?

The second part of this step is to uncover and write down some of those thoughts and feelings. Write down your secret thoughts of who you *know* you really are or who you wish you were to the world. Also, write down the names of anyone you admire and why you admire them.

Step Two

Make a list of positive statements about being enough. No critical, negative statements. Only loving, kind, and compassionate words.

Some examples of these statements are:

I am enough.
I am beautiful enough.
I am full, thin, or fit enough.
I love enough.
I am strong enough.
I am smart enough.
I am whole and complete at this moment.
I am perfect just as I am.
I love big.
I am totally enough in the package, with all these flaws (*name the flaws*).
I am significant.
I have a gift.

I matter.

I am lovable.

I am here for a reason.

Whether you believe in the good or bad, you are always going to be right. You can fool the brain to believe whatever you tell it, and it will manifest whatever it is. So, why not use positive words instead of negative?

I read a sentence someone once wrote: "Don't speak about what is. Speak about what you want things to be, and what you think and speak will come to you."

Your mind does not care what you tell it—good, bad, healthy, or unhealthy. It will start to give you more of whatever is in it. Always make it good and healthy.

Write it all down and repeat it out loud to yourself several times a day.

At first, it will feel like you are lying to yourself. It's okay. Who you really and truly are is good and perfect, loving and kind, and enough, just as you are. You do not have to change. You just need to accept the flaws that come along with the picture of the good you have drawn for yourself.

So, go ahead and start telling yourself amazing things about your amazing self. You will begin to feel these things become a reality.

I remember when I first did this. I called it my "sleep tape." I would say my positive statements while on my treadmill, and I didn't believe most of them. But I kept at it over and over. I felt silly. I felt like a fraud and that it was all a lie. Then, at night, I would put my headphones on and listen as I slept.

Well, today, when I look at those statements, I actually believe them to be true, even though I genuinely thought they were lies and that I didn't deserve them at another time in my life.

It will happen to you too. Just trust the process and *take action*!

Step Three

Practice your own form of meditation, or what I like to call "quiet silence," preferably in a place where you can be quiet. Do something intentionally, like going for a long walk, sitting and drinking that favorite hot drink, guided meditation maybe, or engrossed in reading a book. It can be anything that quiets your mind and helps you be aware of a world bigger than you.

When you become intentional about doing those things every day to get into that quiet space, all kinds of fantastic things start to happen. Awareness begins to take over things that can change your life today and tomorrow. What do I mean by that? Well, people, ideas, and things come into our life, and we will be able to "see" them. We will be aware of them like magic, and we start to expect things to pop up—things that appear through magic, fate, or an unknown force that we don't quite understand.

We need to spend time in this quiet space so we can tap into unknown aspects of life—the awareness of what we can't really explain with words.

You must start somewhere—even with five minutes a day. As you move forward with your days, awareness of a thought or a beautiful scene or the smell of an amazing flower will fill your being, and you will experience the profound wonder of what is to be *for me*. What am *I* here for? What is *my* purpose?

You will get out of the 'I am not enough' space into those of 'I want to be more,' 'I want to be enough,' 'I want to learn what it's all about,' and 'I want it now!'

The journey has been ongoing for me, but it is an exciting adventure. I'm beginning to realize that the "hard" and "dark" times in life are when I can learn the most and begin to fly in the right direction, and trust in the process of life, growth, and love.

So, I wish for you this day to find that quiet space and just listen. The still quiet voice inside of you will sound through just a whisper of a thought. Notice it, and take action.

You will never be sorry you took those moments for yourself. I hope you find yourself living the truth of who you are and be able to say with belief, "I AM ENOUGH!"

BIOGRAPHY

Ann Riedy is a retired registered nurse who set aside her career and dedicated her energies to entrepreneurship. This allowed her to become a business owner in her early thirties. She feels the most important aspect of success is ongoing personal growth and development. Ann started creating her own stories and expressing the world through her eyes when she was very young. She started writing blog posts and sharing her stories on her social media sites. Her unique and engaging writing style taps into the minds and hearts of all who read her work. Ann lives and works out of her home in Eastern Montana. She spends her free time enjoying walks along the river and going on adventures with her grandchildren.

Connect with Ann Riedy via https://linktr.ee/annriedy

CHAPTER 2

JOURNEY TO SUCCESS

By Matt Morris

As a speaker and coach for the past twenty years, I've been blessed to help several thousand people become full-time entrepreneurs with hundreds in the six-figure range and over fifty documented million-dollar earners.

It's also rewarded me with a lifestyle that I never would have imagined as a boy. If you would have told me I'd be a millionaire at twenty-nine, earn eight figures in my thirties and generate several billion in sales, all while adventuring to over eighty countries by my early forties; I wouldn't have believed you.

I also never imagined I'd be blessed with a career that fills me up with such immense levels of fulfillment and significance, knowing that I've been able to assist so many others in achieving what most would consider "boundless" levels of success.

The question I'm asked all the time is . . . How?

In asking that question, most people are looking for tactics and strategies. And I'll admit, early in my coaching days, I focused my mentorship almost solely on teaching the how-tos.

Unfortunately, that made me a pretty lousy coach.

I'd give them the tactics that allowed me to become a superstar salesperson, run a multi-million dollar company, or speak powerfully from stage.

My students would apply the how-tos and come back frustrated with mediocre improvements at best.

What I failed to realize in my early coaching days is a quote from the late Brian Klemmer that says, "If how-tos were enough, we'd all be rich, skinny, and happy."

As we explore the secrets to experiencing boundless levels of success, we must first examine what keeps us bound to our current situation.

Hint: It's NOT a lack of tactics and strategies.

With a quick google search, you can find hundreds of YouTube videos and blog posts that will teach you the strategies to having six-pack abs. The reason most don't have that six-pack isn't that they don't know the how-tos.

When it comes to making your goals a reality, whether that be to have a sexy body, to become a top sales leader in your company, to start your own business, or any other worthwhile dream, the ONLY thing holding you back from achieving that goal is your mental programming.

The challenge most face in achieving a grand visionary future for themselves is the fact that it runs so completely contrary to their current vision, or identity, that's running them now.

Your current identity is made up of the beliefs you currently hold to be true about yourself. It's essentially how you genuinely see yourself.

Your personal identity subconsciously influences every decision and action you make (or don't make), thus influencing the level of success you're able to achieve.

If your personal identity is that of someone who is out of shape or overweight, you may go on streaks where you eat right and exercise vigorously, but you tend to always shift right back into your old ways. Irresistible cravings, lethargy, sleeping in, etc., are somehow always overpowering your desire to be fit.

Why is that the case?

You'll want to write this down.

The Law of Commitment and Consistency

The law of commitment and consistency says that we will remain committed to remaining consistent with who we genuinely believe we are.

That being true, we must understand that in order to change our results, we have to change the beliefs we have about ourselves.

Let's take a deep dive into beliefs.

Take a look at the middle three letters of the word "beliefs," and what word do you see?

LIE

Consider for a moment that the story (the beliefs) you've been telling yourself about who you are as a person are simply lies you've made up.

Stories you may have accepted as "fact" like you're:

- Shy
- Self-conscious
- Lacking self-confidence
- Not a morning person
- Afraid of public speaking
- Not a good communicator
- Not as smart as the others

Would it be empowering to know that any of the negative beliefs above, along with countless others, are nothing more than lies you created subconsciously through a belief-building process you went through and didn't even know you were going through it?

What makes me so certain these "character traits" are lies? Because I had all of those beliefs about myself that I once accepted as fact.

Today, if you told me I was any of those things, I would laugh in your face because it would be completely absurd in my mind to accept any of those as true.

If you're willing to take a journey with me, I'll show you how I literally rewrote my entire identity from a broke, scarcity-filled, self-conscious young man into a confident and powerful multi-millionaire.

I'm here to tell you that whatever limiting beliefs you've created for yourself are absolute and total crap. I'm proof of it and many of those I've mentored for the past twenty years are proof of it.

I don't know what lies about yourself you've accepted as fact, but I know beyond a shadow of a doubt that, at your core, you are not a bad communicator, you are not unworthy of finding love, you are not a failure, you are not destined to always struggle, or any other negative belief.

Whatever they might be, you have the power to change those disempowering beliefs that serve only to limit the amount of success and personal fulfillment you experience.

If your current beliefs are what determine your success, the big question becomes how do you change your beliefs to create the results you want?

Before we answer that question, you first need to understand what shapes your beliefs in the first place. What has caused you to hold the beliefs that you do? Understanding where they came from will help you change them.

The belief building process you went through to come up with the beliefs you currently hold to be true have been shaped by three main factors:

1. Experiences
2. External programming
3. Internal programming

Experiences:

Every experience you've ever been through has been forever deposited and stored somewhere in your subconscious mind.

Maybe you were teased as a kid in school because you stuttered, and now you believe you're a poor communicator. Maybe you were laughed at in class as a kid for giving the wrong answer, and you took on a belief that you're not as smart as the other kids. Maybe you made a few horrible business choices when you were first starting out, and now you think you're lousy in business.

Whether you've realized it before now or not, those deposits were the first major factor that gave you the foundation of your identity.

Here's the way it works . . .

An event happens and then you make up a story (a belief) about what that event means.

Most of us tend to create a negative meaning based on what we perceive to be a negative experience. We create a victim story— I'm not loved because my parents abused me or left me. I'm a terrible business person because I failed for five years. People are not trustworthy because my business partner stole from me (all personal stories I made up at one point).

Think about some examples from your past. Can you think of some examples of events where you created a negative belief?

Real power comes from understanding that nothing has meaning until we give it meaning.

Events are neutral. It's the story we make up from the event that holds all the power. Rather than the victim story you may have been running in your mind, how can you create a new and empowering meaning based on that experience?

Understand—you have the power to choose. Victim or Victor. Which will it be?

External Programming:

Whether you want to believe this or not, you've been programmed.

Your parents programmed you as a child to believe certain things about yourself, other people, money, religion, and many other things.

The school system, your friends, the media, television, and other factors have programmed you to believe many of the things you do today.

Some of this programming has likely been healthy and gotten you to where you are and built you into the person you are today. Unfortunately, we also all have some less than empowering beliefs, and associated fears, that we've adopted as well from that external programming.

By the time you were two years old, you heard the word no thousands of times more than you heard the word yes. It's no wonder so many people, when presented with an opportunity to start a business or take on a challenge, are paralyzed with fear and are hesitant to take action.

At some point in your life, you've most likely faced a moment where someone said something negative to you or doubted your ability, without even meaning to. For a lot of people, that first comes from their parents and family members.

The things that people say to you, whether they intentionally mean harm or not, can profoundly shape who you are—*but only if you let it.* You obviously can't go back into the past and change the negative things you've heard, but you can make the decision right now to no longer let those things define you.

You can recognize that what someone says about you has no basis in reality unless you *choose* to believe it. It's a choice. A choice you can start making right now, today, to say **no more**.

Internal Programming:

More than your experiences and more than the voices of the people around you, the greatest and most powerful way your beliefs are shaped is from your internal programming. Thankfully, it's also the mechanism you have the most control over.

Every word that comes out of your mouth and every thought that comes out of your mind serves as a programming tool. Those thoughts and words get entered into your subconscious mind and then work to create your habitual routines and mental thought patterns.

Psychologists who study brain science agree that your subconscious mind is infinitely more powerful than your conscious mind. The subconscious is the driving force behind your belief system and your identity.

The subconscious mind has a goal that can serve you negatively or positively. That goal is to keep you in line with your identity. Remember the law of commitment and consistency?

If, based on your regular programming, you tell yourself you're broke, you're tired, and you suck as an entrepreneur, your subconscious mind figures out a way to keep you consistent with that programming.

If, however, you continually tell yourself you're wealthy, you're energized, and you're an amazing entrepreneur, your subconscious mind begins doing everything in its power to create *that* reality.

Here's the best way to understand it.

Whatever you say about yourself makes it more true.

If you say, *"I'm an idiot,"* you become more of an idiot. If you say, *"I'm a genius,"* you become more of a genius.

Your consistent programming creates your identity.

Here's the trick; your subconscious mind does not know the difference between the truth and a lie. It simply does its best to carry out exactly what you've programmed it to believe.

So when you say, "I'm sexy, I'm confident, I'm a millionaire," your conscious mind might be telling you you're full of it, but your subconscious mind, which is where the true power lies, will take that as a command and start working out a way for you to be all of those things.

The key to reprogramming your subconscious and changing your deep-seeded beliefs is to change your deposits. You do this by constantly filling your subconscious mind with empowering, uplifting, and motivating thoughts and words.

If you continually profess what you don't want, or focus on the things you don't have or aren't, then you actually attract more of that negativity and continue to reinforce more of that personal identity. **What you focus on expands.**

BIOGRAPHY

Author of the international bestseller, *The Unemployed Millionaire*, Matt Morris began his career as a serial entrepreneur aged eighteen. Since then, he has generated over $1.5 billion through his sales organizations, with a total of over one million customers worldwide. As a self-made millionaire and one of the top internet and network marketing experts, he's been featured on international radio and television and spoken from platforms to audiences in over twenty-five countries around the world. And now, as the founder of Success Publishing, he co-authors with leading experts from every walk of life.

Contact Matt Morris via http://www.MattMorris.com

CHAPTER 3

THE PERSON YOU COULD HAVE BEEN

By Steve Moreland

If Fate's blood-stained cauldron has not found your life yet, she's hiding just over the horizon, waiting until you're at your most vulnerable. So if you're willing to listen to someone that knows about life's ash heap, I'll share the Lessons I learned *after* I failed my Test. The lessons focus on our thinking. More specifically, about how thinking differently empowered me to *thrive* where most cannot imagine surviving. I promise not to waste your time with fluffy bullshit or rah-rah! Just the mental tools what worked, that brought me across a desert wilderness of 5,544 days.

May the following battle-tested advice return you from your <u>seemingly impossible cauldron</u> ***"tested—and found not wanting."***

We Texans pride ourselves on our Code. Toughness is Rule #1. And it means *"no tears allowed."* See, our cult-like indoctrination begins the moment we are born. And the other Spartan rules include: *do only BIG things*, especially if others say it can't be done; *rub some dirt on it* because blood and scars prove your worth; and *do Right*, even if the Lord God, himself, threatens you to do otherwise!

Brutal. Absolutely! But definitely the kind of folks you'd want covering your back in a fight. It's a belief carved deep in our soul—that there simply is NO FREE LUNCH. It is a creed rooted in commitment and perseverance, summed up in one word. Grit!

The standard we have to carry begins early. At age twelve, I started *"earning my worth."* My phone rang off the wall with grass-cutting jobs in the Texas infernos called summer because my dad drilled me to do what everyone else is afraid of, to deliver results beyond expectations. Just self-disciplined results! No excuses.

I went right to corporate America after graduating with academic scholarships – working for three Fortune 500 companies before I was 24. At twenty-five I was in charge of my own brokerage firm in Dallas. By thirty, I'd made it to millionaire status, flew in private jets, brokered 9-figure deals from European castles, banked in numbered Swiss accounts, and spoke on international stages raising millions for venture capital deals.

Ballistic was my term for the vertical climb I experienced. Simultaneously serving as vice president of offshore operations for a boutique hedge fund, CEO of a 58-office tax and wealth management firm, and co-principal of a SaaS startup. I couldn't afford the luxury of sleep. And part of every month, I lived near my office in the banking district of Nassau, Bahamas, acting as the vice president of business development for a middle eastern banking syndicate.

Occasionally, I woke up at a place my then-wife and children called home. It was there that I slowed down enough to rub some of that Texas dirt on my hand tremors from sleeping only on those overseas flights. I was stumbling forward just to maintain the pace. There was something wrong but I could not risk failing the mission. My Dad's standing orders were crystal: *"You can rest when you're dead!"* And this belief came from his creed that a man only earns a medal on his gravestone if he dies "in combat."

Well, I failed to become a "lifer" in the Corps, so I determined that I was going to achieve whatever most would call impossible. I believed in his invincibility! And after eighteen years of his Marine- style bootcamp, I feared only one thing, **"meeting the person I could have been!"**

So, when Fate's blood-stained hurricane came for me, I was Ready. Ready to blindly march into Hell itself. But after the first few years, I felt more like the Greek myth of Sisyphus who was sentenced to pushing a boulder up the mountain every damn day and then waking up the next morning to find it at the bottom again. I remember thinking to myself, "Maybe God is *not* good" after feeling soul-crushing agony for the first time. Real pain that made me wish I could just die and get it over.

I'll admit, all that invincibility crap did NOT work. And I'm painfully embarrassed to admit that I found myself wallowing in my self-pity after losing absolutely everything and feeling abandonment by all I loved. I had succumbed to that state of a *victim.* And you know what, that Texas dirt did NOT fix the wounds I'd caused my family for the undeserved trials and tribulations my bull-headed foolishness caused.

Though I was brought up with my dad's relentless Texan and Marine Corp code of conduct mixed with my mom's Christian beliefs, the devasting pain caused me to question their beliefs. Sitting in the ash heap of my life like the Bible's character Job, I commenced to blaming God for not protecting us from the horror that imprisoned us. I begged and even prayed for an instant release of misery, even raising my fist in anger and shouting "You're *NOT* a good god!"

I just wanted that magical snap of a finger and everything to be like it used to be. But genie-like fixes never happen, do they. Why? Because strength is *not* forged in luxury and comfort. Medals do not get pinned to your chest for holding hands and singing "Kum Ba Yah."

The struggle to endure real agony, to eat suffering, and know your pain so intimately that you name her has a purpose. You see, it took time for me to get over my self-entitlement in order to face my demons and do the most excruciating thing I'd ever done. Realizing that I could not change the past or erase what my mistakes had cost my family, I had to make a decision: either continue to blame others and wallow in self-pity or use the hell I was inside to forge a better version of me!

In school, we're first taught the lesson that prepares us for the test. But, in life, we face the Test first; later, we learn the Lesson.

The grade is what we become through it all. It's pass or fail. And yes, hell is when you meet that person you could have been. It means rising again and again within the blood-stained cauldron of Fate. Only this repeated discipline distinguishes the few from the many, the extraordinary from the ordinary. The worthy from the worthless.

But that person you could have been is only Hell if he or she stands better than you chose to become! **Hell, then, is meeting the *better* person you could have been.**

Like I promised in the beginning, what follows WILL take you through any hell. And you will arrive on the other side, *"tested – and found not wanting."*

Let's begin with a question: "Have you ever been really curious about something—to the point of obsession?"

Since I was a kid, I wanted to unravel this thing called thinking. I reasoned to myself that if I could only understand how the few we call "great" actually thought, I might be able to be like them and make the world a little bit better. Because, for the most part, they are human just like me. The only difference is that they *see things differently* in their minds.

Personal development "coaches" blather about managing our thinking. It is THE key, agreed. But it's not enough to know *what* to do. We've got to know *how* to do it. It's the subtle and often <u>hidden difference between learning science without the art of knowing how it applies to real-world situations</u>. Most of these "well-meaning" coaches deserve an "A" for science but an "F" in art. Never earning a medal from within Fate's blood-stained cauldron means their theories can get you to one destination – that chance to meet the person you could have been.

Here's an example of a coach with earned rank, Dr. Viktor Frankl – author of *Man's Search For Meaning.* Frankl didn't just survive six years of Nazi concentration camps, he changed the world forever with his discovery of how we create meaning through our imagination.

Better thinking creates better doing. And better doing creates a better being.

Frankl forced me to think. I mean really think. And all of a sudden, what Professor Eli Goldratt wrote in *The Goal* became crystal clear. "If we continue to do what we have done, which is what everybody else is doing, we will continue to get the same *unsatisfactory* result." But I asked myself, isn't that what we do so very often - more of what everyone else has done and then expecting a different outcome?

We are what we've done, right? So, aren't our own actions - what we *do* - that creates who we *become*? In short, "doing creates being." So, who we are today – our being, is a product of our past doings? Becoming someone better can only happen by doing differently. And differently results from the seed of the thoughts in our imagination.

Because I wanted a different future – one that honored the sacred by making the world better, I could no longer afford to think like I used to, or like everyone else. Maybe you're brighter than me and already know this. But for me, this realization was the Eureka! And in that realization, I felt something deep inside like lightning.

If my prior thinking caused my current doings (my actions and habits that are known as my reality), **then why couldn't I change my future by changing the way I was thinking?**

Socrates (Greek philosopher 470 B.C.) taught a Secret passed through his student Plato to his student Aristotle (Greek philosopher 384 B.C.). Aristotle planted this Secret into the mind of a 13-year-old prince. This Secret method of thinking changed the ancient world.

At 16 years of age, the prince led his cavalry at the Battle of Chaeronea, decimating a supposedly unbeatable enemy. At 20 years of age, he became king of Greece, marched his army towards Persia, solved the riddle of the Gordian Knot, and destroyed any that opposed.

At 24, he captured the supposedly unconquerable city of Tyre. At 25, he became Pharaoh of Egypt and then returned to the desert near modern-day Babylon to lead his 50,000-man army against a force exceeding 500,000 led by the Persian emperor Darius. Charging into the front line on his legendary black stallion Bucephalus, he achieved the impossible and became emperor of the known world.

By age 30, he had created the largest empire in history. Today, he's still studied in war colleges for his battlefield genius, ethical governance, and unrivaled valor.

The Secret thought? "Be as you wish to seem."

The Result? One *impossible* difficulty after another - CRUSHED!

His Name? Alexander

How is he remembered? Alexander—the Great!

In school, we're first taught the lesson that prepares us for the test. But, in life, we face the Test first; later, we learn the Lesson.

Here's my experience. The Lessons learned *after* the Test lead to better actions—which lead to becoming a better being, right? That means that tests uncover our weaknesses so that we can learn greater lessons. What and who we become through the Tests reflects our grade in life.

If we're honest, we'll admit that we often create our own storms. And then we blame others when we must endure them. But if we use the agony, we find something called grit. Grit is commitment bathed in love to become better than we were the day before. It's a relentless dedication to rise—to become better, stronger, and wiser. It's a refusal to quit, even when we feel we can't get up again.

The question is, will we? Will we persist after the problems that were caused by our poor thinking – and the results that followed? Or will we just quit due to the fear of failing and the probability that life won't be easy?

Being *"tested and found not wanting"* means we'll certainly be scarred from one battle after another. But the scars reflect rank, defining how many times we returned to the cauldron instead of hiding and waiting to be rescued by the God that's testing us.

It may be cliché, but our very thinking sparks our every action. Put another way, our doings, added together over time, construct our being - *what* and *who* we become.

Do we dishonor the Sacred, settling for what everybody else is doing and continuing to get their same *unsatisfactory* results?

Or do we **think better**, in order to **do better**, so that we could **be better**?

We become what we choose to be. This is the Secret. My gift to you, as Aristotle long ago shared with Alexander, "be[come] as you wish to seem."

Now you know that Hell is NOT meeting the person you could have been.

Hell is meeting the *better* person you could have been.

BIOGRAPHY

A native Texan, Steve Moreland is known for two things. Dedicated practice. And success. Success equates to one's level of practice. So he really does only one thing. His Rubicon system teaches how to perform the common under uncommon conditions. Motivated by the Latin creed FORTES FORTUNA ADIUVAT – "Fortune favors the brave," his mission is to deliberately cause affirmative outcomes that would not have occurred otherwise.

Connect with Steve via https://linktr.ee/steve_moreland

CHAPTER 4

INVESTING IN OTHERS

By Alan Cutting

I've always believed I was born for greatness. My dreams have always been big. My goals have always been on a grand scale. I enjoy the finer things in life. I attended an event when I was sixteen. There were over ten thousand attendees and one man standing at the front of the arena. I remember all he did was speak for two or three days about basic relationship conflicts and living in balance by following the integrity of God's teaching. At the end of the seminar, the speaker drew the most remarkable pastel picture. During the seminar, I thought to myself, "I can do this. I want to do this." The exhilaration of becoming a successful speaker and leader became the focal point of my life.

I knew I was intelligent and had within me what it took to become a successful leader. However, I was born into a broken, dysfunctional family. The deck was stacked against me from the beginning. My father was absent and my mother an alcoholic; I pretty much lived on the street. Don't get me wrong: I had a roof over my head and food on the table. But without any parental supervision, I spent years roaming the streets during the day and into the night. As a mischievous teenager, I was wasting away my life's dreams.

During my early years, I took the bull by the horns and became an effective leader at a young age. The future looked promising. At the age of seventeen, I already conquered a few enormous challenges. Along with the few things I mentioned previously, I nearly severed my right arm from a go-cart accident, limiting the use of my prominent hand and arm for the rest of my life. Despite all the surgeries and life changes it brought to my future, I continued to press on, stay on top of life, and prove that I could overcome any challenge. However, I wasn't prepared for what came next. Out of the blue, without any warning, reason, or explanation, I began having grand mal seizures. I did not know how to deal with this, and no one had any answers. I wasn't prepared for this kind of roadblock. Moreover, I wasn't ready for the loss and defeat it brought to my life.

When I was seventeen years old, there was a pastor of a church, Lon Eckdahl. He took me under his wing and invested in my life. Lon became a father figure, mentor, and my friend. He reached out to me and took me into his home when I was sleeping in my car at the age of seventeen. He spent time with me and showed me that he cared . . . truly cared! He did things along with me as a dad would do for his own son. He taught me and still continues to teach me valuable life lessons. He showed me that he truly believed in me and cared about me. When I was brought to my knees because of these seizures, Lon, unbeknownst to me, had a prominent university reach out to me (through his connections) and enroll me as a student. I had never taken the SAT or ACT, and I entered college with a GPA of 1.95. I must say that I not only graduated with my bachelor's degree but went on to receive two master's degrees. All because of a man who unselfishly gave of himself to invest in a teenager who he believed had a promising future in the leadership of others. In Lon Eckdahl was true leadership: Servant Leadership. As I grew and matured, Lon became one of my closest friends and confidants.

Lon, my father figure and mentor, was and is an amazing leader and taught me about the characteristics and qualities of great leadership:

1. Communication
2. Integrity
3. Self-Awareness
4. Ability to Delegate
5. Give Respect
6. Empathy
7. Gratitude
8. Teachable

But as I grew, the perils of my dysfunctional past and unanswered questions regarding my seizure disorder began to creep into my behavior, and low and behold, I destroyed everything I touched. I was like a farmer with a black thumb. The medications I was given sent me into a bipolar state for over a decade. My wife divorced me. My second wife died. The leader inside me disappeared. It vanished. Then one day, I unintentionally hurt the very person who practically laid down his life for me—Lon Eckdahl. I will never forget the look on Lon's face and the words he angrily spoke to me. That dagger was deep in my heart. And realizing that it was me that put it there, I thought I lost my friend forever.

It took some time, but during my thirties, my medication changed. No more barbiturates. No more bipolar behavior. I felt like a new man. So, I decided to take an inventory of my life and a look at my future. I began to ask myself, "Did I destroy my life? Is there any hope for my future?" I decided to do one of the hardest things that I needed to do. With all humility and sincerity, I reached out to my father figure and mentor, Lon. I flew to his home in Oregon. I poured out my soul, asked for forgiveness, and made restitution to reconcile our broken relationship. Like the true servant leader he was, Lon welcomed me, forgave me, and once again began to invest in me with his words of wisdom and encouragement. I felt that I had ruined my life and any future I may have had. Lon assured me that I had the ability and the talent to turn things around and that all things are possible—that it was never too late. I left Oregon with the confidence of knowing I had someone who believed in me and was always willing to invest his life in me—for who I was and what I do.

When I came home, my new wife and I created a highly successful promotional products corporation by implementing Biblical principles like integrity and honesty. We sold flags, banners, trade show displays, and specialty items. I traveled to Europe and began teaching and giving seminars, becoming more well-known than I thought possible. Finally, I began my own teaching ministry. Today, I reach out to several thousand people worldwide through my weekly program.

I learned that the goal of leadership is to bring out the best in people through respect, care, and continual support for their success.

I took a hard look at the great leaders of history:

1. Jesus of Nazareth

2. Moses the Deliverer

3. Martin Luther

4. George Washington

5. Mahatma Gandhi

6. Nelson Mandela

7. Mother Teresa

8. Billy Graham

Then I took another hard look at successful business leaders of our time:

1. Warren Buffett

2. Bill Gates

3. Izhak Ben Shabbat

4. Matt Morris

A common element that made each of these people great leaders is that they invested in others in order to help develop their "investees" to become good leaders. This is what made them great. You see, development matters!

A few years ago, I decided that I wanted a residual income. So, my wife and I jumped into a home "relationship marketing" business. Actually, my wife thought I was crazy since we already had a successful business with several employees. Luckily for me, though she didn't trust this type of business, my wife believed in me. Starting was easy. However, life happens, of course! Just a few months into the business, my wife's mother passed away. Then her father broke his hip and moved in with us. We soon bought some property. We designed the plans for a new house, and my father, who was a custom home builder, came to live with us and helped build our beautiful new home. During this time, when the house was not quite finished, my father fell and died. So, we had to finish building ourselves. Then my father-in-law also died. All this happened in a matter of four years. Needless to say, our new home business took a hit due to the lack of time we invested in it. I watched others pass me by in the ranks. Then as luck would have it, we had someone—a high-ranked leader and seven-figure earner on our team—who decided to invest in our success. We hung on their words and examples. Then, we decided to implement some of our own ideas and methods. Without too much effort, we began to rise in ranks, and sure enough, money started flowing into our bank account. A very high-ranking individual told me something the other day: "Have I arrived? Not a chance. There's a big world out there to conquer, and I am just getting started."

In conclusion, if there is any wisdom I can pass on to you through my life's story, it is this: learn to develop leaders in your organization and lifestyle. Through my leadership, teaching, and mentorship, I have seen students, pastors, colleagues, and many others rise in their leadership potential. I guess the latest term used is "pay it forward." I said this earlier and feel the need to reiterate. The goal of leadership is to bring out the best in people through respect, care, and the continued support for their success.

We've heard it said so many times that to build success, build leaders. Now we have the buzzwords "Servant Leadership." What does all that mean? How do we do this? It's about investing in others. If you want to be a great leader, be an example of servant leadership and invest your heart and time into those around you. It's what and how you invest in others that will make the difference between mediocrity and greatness. It will be the people you invest in who will take you to the top.

BIOGRAPHY

Alan Cutting is the Bible instructor and speaker for The Believer's Journey, a Bible teaching program that broadcasts weekly and reaches thousands of viewers and listeners from various countries. Coming from humble beginnings, Alan Cutting knows what it means to reach for the top just to be struck down. However, Alan is a success story. With the odds against his favor, he kept striving to succeed. Since 2001, Alan has been the operations manager for a successful promotional marketing corporation. He took a small local company, turned it into a national and then international corporation. Previously, Alan has served in the ministry as an Associate Pastor, high school Bible teacher, and Bible professor for a total of twenty-four years. He continues to travel to Europe and speaks to teachers, Christian ministers, and holds seminars on various topics relating to personal relationships. Alan has volunteered his time to help his local community as one of the founders of The Christian Business Chamber of Commerce and has sat on the board of directors for the Better Business Bureau for several years. Alan has earned three master of arts degrees and is presently completing his PhD in Theology. He has authored a book of poetry, Whispers of the Heart. Recently Alan and his wife, Susan, decided to venture into a home-based business to create passive income for their future. Using his past experiences in leadership, integrity, and paying forward the investment into his life from his mentors and leaders, Alan has already become a leader in his organization in a short time while building new and upcoming leaders. His ability to invest in others has been the cornerstone to developing new leaders in every area of his life and work. Read his story. It will truly touch your heart and move you to a new understanding of great leadership.

Connect with Alan Cutting via https://linktr.ee/konakid54

CHAPTER 5

WHY ARE YOU HERE?

By Alan Lowe

Why are you where you are? I am not referring to your current physical location as you read this book. I am asking this question from the perspective of where in your life you are right now. Is your career at the level that you want it to be? Is your relationship with your children what you want it to be? Is your relationship with your spouse the best it can be? How about your relationship with your other relatives and your coworkers? How is your relationship with yourself? What do you honestly think about yourself? If you hold the Christian faith, how is your relationship with God? Are all these aspects of your life really where you want them to be?

More than likely, you are here because you feel that something is missing, something is not quite where you want it to be, or there should be more to life than what you're experiencing. Many people feel that way, and that is what led me here as well. I remember, several years ago, sitting at my desk at work, thinking that what I was doing was not what I wanted to do for the rest of my life. But I had no idea what that would be, and I felt that there was a bigger purpose for why God put me here. After all, I am still here. I knew I liked helping people but could not figure out how I could get to where I wanted to be—wherever that was—or what to do to get there. If you have some of these feelings, it is perfectly natural. All I can say is you have already taken the first step to getting where you want to be. Once you realize that a change is needed, be prepared for opportunities to present themselves. There may be only one, or there may be many, but you must be ready to recognize them. And it is vitally important to keep an open mind. Understanding how you got to where you are right now is the next step.

So how did you get where you are right now? Facing the reality that the decisions and choices you made resulted in you being where you are today is of the utmost importance. If you're still blaming others for where you are, stop reading now, and come back when you face reality because those are the things that have made your life what it is today. It does not matter if everything in your life is exactly where you want it to be. If that's what you think, I suggest you look at yourself from someone else's perspective. The areas you would like to improve on, the fact that you are where you are because of the decisions, actions, and choices you did or did not make, cannot be blamed on anyone else. And yes, there may be instances where external factors you had no control over affected your life, but your responses were your choices.

At some point, you will realize that those choices and the continued struggle for what is missing have a cost. The sooner you value the time spent, the sooner you will make a real commitment. For me, it took quite some time, and the true cost was not understood until many years later. What helped me understand was the realization that I would never have gotten where I am being the person I was. That awakening led me on a path of continued self-improvement. One of my favorite quotes is by Ray Kroc: "As long as you're green, you're growing. As soon as you're ripe, you start to rot."[1] If you are not familiar with Ray Kroc, I suggest you look him up and, like me, you'll know he wasn't talking about tomatoes. With the multiple self-improvement classes and nights away from the family, I was still not getting the results I was expecting.

In my case, I chose to try and keep up with the Joneses over many years and continually looked for "opportunities" that would allow me to achieve what I felt I was missing. At least, that was the story I told myself. I would try (try is the keyword) one thing after another, having some success with my search. Little did I realize the true cost of my search. It was not until one of the people I met at a meeting kept bugging me to check out "this thing" she knew I would like. After several weeks of dodging her and coming up with excuses, I knew she would not stop until I went, so I did. This happened to be one of those opportunities disguised as one thing but completely different from what I expected. I did not even realize it until many months later. While going through what turned out to be a transformational process, I learned who I really was and why I made the decisions that got me where I was. This process was not easy as it required an in-depth look at oneself. If you do this and are honest with yourself (as I was, in my case), it can be very painful. You come to realize that people do not perceive you as you think they do. You learn that your actions or inactions affect people around you in ways you would not intentionally want, and your self-perception takes on a new outlook. So, a portion of the cost was my realization that I was not the person I thought I was or even wanted to be. In fact, I was somewhat ashamed of who I was and why it took me so long to realize it. On the other hand, the benefit was that I did finally realize it and was willing to do something to change.

---

1   "Ray Kroc Quotes," BrainyQuote (Xplore), accessed July 29, 2021, https://www.brainyquote.com/quotes/ray_kroc_130750.

After finally understanding who I really was came the realization of how inconsiderate I had been. I spent all those nights chasing the Jones's, going to meetings and training, and not being with my family. Telling myself that I was doing it for them was not the truth; I had convinced myself that it was. But during that truthful soul-searching as to why I was not where I wanted to be, the worst thing I realized was that I was doing it to avoid conflicts at home, leaving all the problems to my wife. We did not argue or get into fights or anything like that. I mean, how could we? I was never there. I left our family up to her.

My inability to recognize my shortcomings created a tremendous amount of unnecessary strain on our marriage. Had I stepped back and been present to what I was doing, I would not have caused such hardships for my wife and children. In moments like these, we find ourselves wanting the impossible—wanting the ability to turn back the hands of time for a second chance to do things better. That not being possible, we must accept our mistakes, learn from them, become better people, and continue to evaluate how our actions affect others. We are still together after forty-nine years, and I am very thankful we are.

My dad taught me something based on his life experiences. If people cannot trust your word, what can they trust you with? My dad was a communications sergeant and Bronze Star recipient in the Army during WWII, so soldiers' lives literally depended on his words. I gave my word to my wife and to my Creator when we stood at the altar "…until death do you part," and I will never go back on that promise. Nor will I go back on the promise I made to myself to continually improve and consciously be aware of how I am affecting others.

So, these are the reasons for this book. All those times away from my wife and children had another detrimental cost. Years later, one of my grown daughters told me, "You were never there when I needed you." That one left a hole in my soul that I have not found a way to heal. If this book helps one person make a real commitment to change their life and not just use it as an excuse, it accomplishes what I intended. Do not do something that takes time away from your family and only do it half-assed. Your family deserves more. Be the person worthy of the family God has graced you with.

My transformation process has given me many opportunities to become the person I want to be: a person who 'pays it forward' and makes other people's lives better. It took me down a path that allowed me to create a non-profit primarily focused on children. Over the past three years, it has provided Christmas parties for hundreds of children in Liberia who otherwise would have had no Christmas. My fulfillment does not come in monetary form. My fulfillment comes from seeing the joy and smiles on the faces of those I can help and hearing their appreciation. Every day, I make a conscious effort to live a life of gratitude. If we fill our thoughts with gratitude, there is no room for negativity.

Opportunities may be as subtle as refusing to give up your seat on a bus in 1955. Rosa Parks was an African American seamstress in Montgomery, Alabama, and her decision started the Civil Rights movement that changed the country. Or they may be as drastic as the death of Candy Lightner's thirteen-year-old daughter, who a repeat drunk driver killed in 1980 and led to the founding of Mothers Against Drunk Drivers. Or Todd Beamer, an account manager on Flight 93 during September 11, 2001, who helped take down the plane to prevent it from crashing into the Capitol Building.

As they say in Scouting, 'Be Prepared." Know who you are, where you are, where you want to go, and what you are willing to do to get there.

And for those who were nonbelievers and naysayers, I have created a PBB award. It is a plexiglass surgical implant that replaces the belly button. This allows them to walk around and still see where they are going while they have their head up their rectum. And yes, I awarded the first one to myself.

BIOGRAPHY

Alan Lowe is a native Texan and resides in Spring, Texas, just north of Houston. Alan is a successful business executive who has consulted with numerous multimillion-dollar companies throughout the United States. His experience in interpersonal relationships played a vital role in his ability to help those companies achieve their objectives. Alan is a United States Air Force Vietnam veteran, where he received top-secret clearance. He believes in God and country, family, and the American dream. He learned from his father that if people can't trust you for your word, they can't trust you for anything. His mother taught him that if you can't say something nice about somebody, don't say anything. She also taught him the taste of Ivory soap. He has a passion for giving back through the pay-it-forward principle and backs his belief by being the founder and president of his non-profit Helping Hugs For Children and an Advisory Council Member of Soldiers' Angels. He is a graduate of the University of Houston with a bachelor's degree in Business Administration and a graduate of Landmark Worldwide, where he founded the non-profit Helping Hugs For Children. He has held a Series 6 Securities license from the S.E.C. and an Insurance License from the State of Texas. Alan is passionate about self-improvement and can usually be found with a book on this subject and always listening to one while driving. His personal fulfillment comes not from money but from helping others achieve levels in their life they thought were not possible. He enjoys fishing and not catching fish which he is very good at. Alan understands the importance of accepting people for who they are and not wanting them to be somebody else.

Connect with Alan Lowe via https://linktr.ee/alanglowe51

CHAPTER 6

BE A ONER

By Anne Carr

"Be a Oner," my volleyball coach told my team as he handed out our weekly training flyer. We were sitting on the floor after a long practice session. Our sheets were full of quotes, plays, schedules, and information we needed to best represent our state at the National Championships. I had to catch two buses to and from practice that took about four hours out of my day on training days. I was tired, not sure if I deserved to be there, questioning my own ability as a player and wondering how the heck I was going to make all of this work. "Be a Oner," he said. To this day, I still have that flyer.

You know those defining moments, don't you? They are the little things said in passing. They could be from family, friends, and even a stranger. Sometimes, they are off-the-cuff spoken words. It could be a spontaneous word or phrase—the ones that people flippantly say without realizing its significance. But for you, it hits all the right feelings in the moment, and quite possibly, it was spoken at the wrong time as well as the right time. Sometimes, they are positive and mean well; sometimes, they are not. They are the quickly spoken words or brief, fleeting actions that ultimately end up influencing the recipient for life and come back to visit over and over again to remind them. We never know whether the words thrown at us will stick with us like we never truly know the impact *our* words and actions have on others.

I heard and felt those few short words of encouragement deep down to my core. Thirty-six years later, the words that still echo through my head and jump out at me whenever I feel stagnant, when I am struggling to move through an obstacle, looking to break through to the next level, or when stepping out of my comfort zone.

I was eighteen years old and playing volleyball. I was not the tallest, fastest, biggest, strongest, or smartest. Well, we never really are, are we?! There is always someone bigger, better, smarter, prettier, happier, more talented . . . Or is there? I now know that at that time in my life, I certainly thought that everyone around me was. I struggled getting through college because I was unsure where I wanted to go in life. I managed to sink myself into a vicious cycle of skipping classes, thereby getting low grades. So, I would skip class again because I was behind. The circle kept spiralling, and not in a good way. I distinctly remember one of my professors pulled me aside and said to me, 'Don't think you are anyone special. You are only a number and not a pretty face.' I even remember this same professor reading a certain section of my paper out in front of the class and laughing along with the class. He kept my name anonymous, of course, but I remember sinking into my chair, my face burning, and hoping that nobody would know it was my paper. There you have it; those became the defining words that would come up in my mind. I convinced myself I was not smart and fell into self-destruct mode. I'd party late at night and sleep in, feeling like I was not worthy and deserving enough to be in college.

My volleyball kept me on a schedule and mostly kept me out of trouble. Hearing those words from my coach—Be a Oner—helped turn me around and gave me something to look for beyond my current situation. Be a Oner. Always do *one more*. I used this in everything to help get myself back on track. I still do. I began looking for areas where I could do one more good thing for someone. I could be one more good friend for somebody else. When I worked out, I could do one more push-up, one more sit-up, push towards my goals for one more second, minute, hour, or day, depending on what I was aiming for. Now, don't get me wrong, I use this for all areas of my life, including the times I need to rest. It is not possible to be pushing constantly. I know the times I need to use this as motivation as well as the times I need to allow my soul the peace to regroup. I am super competitive, so this helped not only when I was competing against myself but also when I was competing against others with my team. Whatever I needed to do to go beyond was possible when I fell back on these small words of inspiration, which amounted to many breakthroughs.

I have questioned myself moving forward several times, and countless times, I will still ask myself: Where do I start? I tell myself to be a Oner.

I get my body moving to get my mind moving, and I get my mind moving to get my body moving. It's interchangeable—whichever one resonates with you first. I find it depends on the circumstance.

I've found most people question themselves as I did, and yes, to this day, they still do. We're all on a never-ending journey of discovery, with choices being thrown at us every second of every day. As long as we are breathing, this will always remain constant.

I know. I've been there. I still, to this day, tend to overthink, overanalyse, and question whether what I do is important. When I'm stuck in indecisiveness with my next step, I close my eyes and take a deep breath. I become a Oner. I do one more of the "things" I need to do to bring me closer to my goal, purpose, and mission of empowering others. I reach out with one more message of inspiration. I write one more thank you letter. I make one more connection. I validate one more friend who I see giving it their all. I send off one more note of gratitude. I spend one more minute checking in with someone who needs it at that exact moment. I plant one more seed of promise. I send off one more cheer of encouragement. I uplift one more friend. Even when I am tired, I know I can do one more. I give everything *one more*, even when I sometimes feel that these efforts go unnoticed, even when I know that I need that extra nudge of encouragement, and even when I am not feeling it myself. Why do I refuse to quit? Because there are too many people stuck and spiralling downwards like I once was.

As I sat there and listened to my coach encouraging us— me—to be a Oner, I knew that I needed to be a Oner in all areas of my life and use this to launch myself through bigger, stronger challenges and obstacles.

What if my coach had never shared those words of wisdom with me? Where would I be now? Would I have made the starting team? Would I have put in more effort in making the team? Would I have been inspired to make more of an effort in all areas of my life? Would I have used those words to propel myself forward? Would I have shifted my mindset to that of always taking one step forward, or would I have stayed in that place of mediocrity, not knowing how to dig myself out of holes? Would I have held myself back, never truly knowing what I could accomplish if I only exceeded what I thought was my limit? Would I have blown through that comfort zone barrier we all know way too well? We'll never truly know the answers to these questions. However, I know that I can help inspire others by passing on these words of wisdom—words that carried me through my adult life. It's my turn to pass it on.

Truthfully, the only person we are competing with is ourselves. So, make sure to take these words and use them to better yourself.

Do you have big dreams, goals, and visions? Be a Oner to move yourself closer. Read one more minute of that book you love. Do one more rep of that workout program you are on. Reach out to one more friend, so they know they have another option. Offer up one more smile to a stranger. Give one more moment of your time to your mission. Allow yourself one more hour in the morning for your self-care so you can be a better you—for both yourself and your family.

Oh, and one more thing. The beauty of our choices is exactly that. We can choose to make the world a more beautiful place than it is now, one step at a time, beginning with doing one little thing. Then, be a Oner. Do one more thing, no matter how big or small. You will question yourself. It's human nature. However, I know this is true: I know I can do one thing, and I know you can do one thing.

Let's be Oners together!!!

BIOGRAPHY

Anne Carr was born in Broken Hill, Australia, and graduated from Flinders University with a bachelor of arts, double majoring in psychology and sociology. She was a national-level track and field and soccer athlete and an All-Australian volleyball player, receiving a Commonwealth Full Sporting Blue. After graduating, she travelled the world by herself for three and a half years, ending up in Palo Alto, California. Anne has been married for twenty-seven years to her wonderful husband, Gavin, and they have three incredible sons, aged twenty-six, twenty-three, and seventeen. They've owned Stanford Chiropractic Center for over thirty-three years, and Anne has been a beauty industry leader for over seven years. Her goal is to redefine beauty and teach others how to highlight their natural, inner, and unique beauty and stop the comparison game. Anne is a bestselling author and public speaker. She is a Third-Degree Black Belt and currently training in Brazilian Jiu-Jitsu.

Connect with Anne Carr via https://linktr.ee/AnneRachaelCarr

CHAPTER 7

THE NEVER-ENDING BATTLE

By Antwan Winkfield

Introduction

LIFE IS NOT EASY. I'm sure we all can contest. We must learn to be okay with not being okay because life is not perfect, and you will face adversity. Some will encounter more adversities than others, but understand this: how we respond to adversity separates us from others. Will you make excuses and give up without a fight? Will you mope around and be mad at the world? Will you allow the negativity to dictate your attitude and shift your mindset to the point you give up on all your life goals? After reading my chapter, I hope 'giving up' will be the last of your worries, and the will to fight will be automatic whenever faced with misfortune. Here's a favorite saying to get us started: LET YOUR FAITH BE BIGGER THAN YOUR FEARS. My life continues to be a never-ending battle, yet I have achieved significant milestones by maintaining a positive mindset. I want to say my problems are no bigger than anyone else's; the difference is how I respond. My never-ending battle may change your life.

In The Beginning

Unlike most other children enjoying themselves on the playground, I was fighting for my life. My back and shoulders hunched, and every movement caused me to cringe in pain. I could only imagine myself enjoying the gratification of being a normal kid. I remember my mom telling me I cried a lot as a baby. It was unknown at the time, but those were tears of pain. By two years old, doctors confirmed that I inherited severe scoliosis and a fibrocystic disease known as neurofibromatosis. Both disorders have affected my family for generations, but I must have gotten the short straw as I was getting ready to enter the fight of my life.

I was one when my mother realized there was more behind all my crying. One night, during bath time, my mother noticed my spine starting to curve. After seeing a specialist, they discovered the neurofibromatosis was beginning to wrap itself around the upper portion of my spine, and like a python, it was slowly squeezing my vertebra. My spine had grown so weak; one fall could have left me permanently paralyzed. My condition and the outcome were rare. The story was featured in a Children's Mercy Hospital publication. I was the cover story; I thought I was so cool. The article was quoted saying: "Like a Charlie Brown Christmas tree, the weight of his head had pulled the spine over into the shape of a 7, pushing vital organs into cramped quarters." I would undergo my first series of spinal surgeries at the age of two. The surgeons attempted to fuse my weakened vertebrate. Sadly, two years later, the spine overpowered the fusion, and the curve grew worse. If a surgeon could not stop the curve from worsening, I would show more signs of spinal compression, and my body would start shutting down, and life for me would end before it had the chance to start.

The power of GOD is real. Up until this moment, after many failed attempts to slow the curvature, doctors told my mother it would be a miracle if I saw the age of ten, let alone if I ever walked again. My spine was so weak I was now wheelchair-bound. Out of the blue, my family's prayers were answered. Dr. W, an Orthopedic Specialist, was recently placed at Children's Mercy to complete his residency. He stepped in with a game plan that would later give me a chance at life. The goal would be to straighten my spine as much as possible by placing me in a portable traction unit. I spent over ten weeks wearing a halo that connected to a weighted pulley. Once my vertebrae had straightened as much as possible, Dr. W would fuse the bones in place by reinforcing the fusion with metal rods, a bone graft from my pelvis, and a rib. It was a timely process and took a series of surgeries, the outcome of which I have deemed a miracle.

I spent a great deal of my childhood in the hospital. By the age of five, I had undergone over ten operations. I learned at an early age how precious life is. I learned the importance of having faith and staying mentally strong, all while remaining positive. A friend once asked me if I could go back in time, would I change anything? I quickly answered no. Going through everything I had to endure so early in life made me wise beyond my years. Most importantly, I learned one of my essential rules of life: DO NOT WASTE ENERGY WORRYING, ON THINGS BEYOND YOUR CONTROL.

In life, bad things happen no matter what. Why waste energy worrying or getting upset? You will drive yourself insane. Whenever things are beyond your control, focus your energy on being positive and doing everything to better the situation. My situation was beyond my control. So, instead of being mad at the world and giving up, I focused my energy on believing things would get better. I imagined myself out on the playground. I refused to allow negative thoughts to enter my mind. A positive mindset and belief are essential in overcoming adversity. One must believe in the achievable to reach the reachable. The first step is believing.

Adolescence/College Years

1995, I hit a meaningful milestone: I turned ten years old. When I was three years old, my mother was told it would take a miracle for me to reach the age of ten. I was on cloud nine, empowered. Here I stand (even today), just shy of five feet, walking without the need of a wheelchair and more alive than ever. Doctors were amazed. They no longer predicted my life span but now shifted on ways to slow me down. I was always trying to keep up with the other kids, but I did have physical limitations. Trying to get me to slow down was never an easy task. You could always catch me on the basketball court playing with my brothers, cousins, and stepfather. I struggled at times, but I just kept pushing. I can remember one thing I hated growing up was that I was never allowed to play competitive sports. Basketball was one of my favorite sports. Where there is a will, there is a way. In high school, I could not be a part of the team. Physically, my body could not keep up. Determined to be involved, I wanted to earn my varsity letter. I realized my school's mascot was the Mighty Pirates, but yet, we did not have a live mascot, and our basketball games were crazy. I ended up convincing the arts coordinator to make me the school's first mascot. I became a fan favorite, and I got to hang out with the cheerleaders. I was on top of the world. When you want something bad enough, you will find a way. Sometimes, you might have to accept an alternative version of what you originally envisioned. I could not be a high school basketball star, but I could be the official Paseo Pirate.

Another essential rule of life: BELIEVE YOU CAN DO ANYTHING. BE WILLING TO WORK FOR IT, AND DO NOT BE AFRAID TO FAIL. It starts with a choice. Once you make that choice, you have to be all in and determined enough that nothing can deter you. Once I got to high school, I decided and was determined to be in the top ten of my graduating class. At the time, college was not on my radar. My biological father was in prison; my stepfather was not around when I needed that father figured the most. My mother, for whom I'm so thankful, had to be tough, raising boys and having a child with significant health problems. I did not understand it while it was happening, but my mom was the hardest on me. My mom played a crucial role in ensuring she did not baby me so I would not use my handicap as an excuse. I thought she was mean at the time, but I was not treated any differently between her and my family.

It was not until I met Major Brooks, my Junior Reserve Officer Training Corps (JROTC) instructor, in the eighth grade, did I realize college was attainable. Major Books gave all his students hope. He helped me open Pandora's box, and I was ready to conquer the world. I was going to be a first-generation college graduate. I put all my faith in God because I had no idea how I was going to pay for school. I just decided I was going, and nothing would deter me from reaching my goal. 2003 came. There I sat on stage at graduation, ranked #7. I was excited and ready for the next chapter of life. I would soon be packing up and leaving the nest to attend the University of Kansas, home of the Jayhawks.

College was the experience of a lifetime. I was in and out of the hospital with pneumonia every winter but kept fighting. May 2008—graduation day. I was a little guy from the inner city, not the best high school education, with life-threatening health issues, and coming from a broken home. But I just graduated from college! I tell young people that getting into college was the easy part; graduating was the challenge. In 2010, I was admitted to the ICU with pneumonia, H1N1, and a collapsed lung. The situation was emotional. The waiting room was filled with friends and family. You would have thought I was famous. I was not alert during all this as I was in a medically induced coma. Through the grace of God, I pulled through like a champ. Once I was 100 percent, I promised myself to continue my education and get my master's in business administration. I learned that I suffered from Chronic Restrictive Lung Disease. Due to my past back surgeries and the metal rods, my lungs are cramped and unable to expand fully.

I would now have to adapt and get used to being a tracheotomy patient while relying on oxygen and a ventilator. If you ever see me out, I'll be the one pushing a mini cart filled with the equipment I need to assist me in breathing. In 2013, despite all the challenges, I completed my MBA in September. But sadly, I would spend the next five to six months in the hospital as my health took a turn due to tumors pushing against my lung. Over the next eight years, four more operations followed, bringing my total to sixteen surgeries. The ICU was like a second home, but throughout all my battles, I never gave up. I always remained positive. Most of all, I survived.

Are you willing to commit to never giving up without a fight? There will come a time when you will feel overwhelmed; you will feel the world is against you. I am here to tell you everything will be okay. Every day you wake up is a new day to wipe the slate clean. You can decide the type of person you're going to be. Life is about balance; you will have good days and bad ones. You cannot just accept the good, and then the moment you face some difficulty, get mad and want to curse the world. Life is like a storm. Some days, it can get nasty out. But at some point, that storm will come to an end. Meaning, bad times do not last forever. So, if you know this mentally, why not change the way you approach adversity?

I not only speak of this idea of living life with a positive mindset, but I also live it every day. The moment I committed to having a positive approach to life, the hard times became easier to manage. As I bring my chapter to a close, I'm proud to say, at thirty-six years old, I can count on my two hands the number of times I allowed myself to be stressed, upset, or unhappy. Every day I wake up, I choose to be positive. Every time I have to be hospitalized, I could choose to be negative, hate the world, and have a horrible attitude. But it only makes the tough times more challenging. If you focus on the hurt, you will continue to suffer. If you focus on the lesson, you will continue to grow. A positive mind is your key to success. What will you choose?

BIOGRAPHY

Antwan Winkfield is an inspiring individual. He inspires people daily without even knowing. Born and raised in Kansas City, MO, Antwan graduated from Paseo Academy, a performing arts high school. The odds were against him: facing major health issues and growing up in the inner-city. Antwan was in a constant battle for his life. Giving up was not a part of his plan. Upon graduating at the top of his class, Antwan left for the University of Kansas. He earned a bachelor's in social work and became a first-generation college graduate. Antwan spent five years working with juvenile delinquents and children living in the system before continuing his education at Baker University, earning a Master's in Business Administration. Antwan is unique in his ability to empower others and his will and determination to succeed despite his life complications. Everyone who meets Antwan will walk away a better person.

Connect with Antwan Winkfield via
https://linktr.ee/workingtowardsadream

CHAPTER 8

SCREW IT, LET'S DO IT!

By Barb Naisby

This book by Richard Branson did not exist when I started my entrepreneurial journey, but I think it was written just for me! "Screw It, Let's Do It" has become my mantra.

Did you ever have your career path mapped out for you? Did you fall into line because it was expected of you? Did you lack self-esteem because it had been drummed into you that your opinion was worthless, nobody would be interested in you and that you had to do as you were told, regardless of your own thoughts? That was me!

I always thought I wanted to be a teacher, and my mother wanted that for me too, provided that I went to an all-girls Catholic college. But, when I started my training, I discovered I hated teaching with a passion. I also knew, without the shadow of a doubt, that I would be in deep shit when my mother found out I'd dropped out of college.

This was the first time I actually stood up to her about following my own path rather than one she dictated, and boy, there were some spectacular arguments! I wouldn't back down, and she wouldn't speak to me. So, I got a job, found an apartment, and moved out to the sounds of "Don't you come crying to me when you have no money." I would rather have starved than admit defeat!

I guess I honestly didn't know what made me tick at the ripe old age of twenty, but looking back, I can see the determined, ambitious, absolutely focused person I am today. Oh, did I forget to mention bloody-minded too?

I'd been with my boyfriend, Dave, since I was fifteen. So, we decided to get married. One more thing to add to my mother's "Mad at Barb" list. She probably did have a point that we were too young, not to mention that I had to support Dave through his last two years at dental school. But I'm proud to say we proved her wrong. We're still together today, and this journey really belongs to both of us, not just me.

Dave had only been qualified for eight months when we got the opportunity to buy a rundown practice in Sunderland, England, from a retiring dentist, Tommy Mustard. Did we baulk at the idea? Did either of us consider our lack of experience in the dental or business world? Nope. The thought never crossed our minds! So off we went to see Tommy's bank manager to borrow money to buy the practice. Sheer bloody cheek, because we had neither collateral nor an account with that bank, and Dave still had a student overdraft to repay. Our bravado paid off, though. The bank manager took a shine to us, lent us the deposit on a short-term loan, and set up a mortgage for the remainder.

I didn't know it then, but that was the start of my entrepreneurial journey. We decided that Dave would concentrate on dentistry while I would learn everything I could about making our practice stand out from the crowd, which was a pretty tough task given the stringent rules of the General Dental Council, the dental controlling body. We were in trouble with them more than once!

Back in the seventies, in the UK, when you qualified from dental school, 99.9 percent of graduates went to work as subcontractors to the National Health Service. You provided your own premises, your own equipment, your own staff, and your own materials. In return, you got to churn out factory-style dentistry on a fee-per-item basis. The only way to break even was to churn out multiple dentistry items at a rapid-fire pace and employ other dentists who could do the same. That's just the way it was.

In 1988, some friends of ours had moved from Sunderland to the Scottish Highlands, and we felt they had a much better quality of life up there. So, we decided to up sticks and move before the kids got to senior school age. Within three months, the house and the business were sold, and in August 1988, David joined a practice in Hilton, Inverness.

This practice was a 100 percent NHS business, and the pressures of seeing thirty-five to forty patients a day eventually took their toll on Dave, who completely crashed and burned in September 2000. Unfortunately, we had just taken out a large bank loan to buy out Dave's partner and completely refurbish the practice and equipment. As business manager, I had lost my only high-achieving dentist and was forced to borrow money from my sister to make the loan repayments and keep the business afloat. Thanks again, Pam!

I'd seen the writing on the wall as far as Dave's mental health and ability to keep working at this pace were concerned, and I'd already made plans to initiate a major change. Just before Dave had to take time off work, I had booked myself for a course in London called "The Dental Entrepreneur." We were broke, but I decided to go as the course and flight were already paid for. It was here that I was introduced to two mentors who helped me change the path of our business and our lives.

The first mentor was Chris Barrow of The Dental Business School, who offered a two-year coaching program to teach dental teams how to move from NHS dentistry to private dentistry and learn how to run a dental business instead of a dental factory. During this event, Chris spoke at length about a crazy Australian dentist named Paddi Lund, who was destined to become our second mentor.

I arrived home with a brochure detailing The Dental Business School's program, which was going to cost £375 per quarter (about $600 at the time). I carefully cut out all the references to cost from the large presentation brochure (remember we were broke?) and asked Dave to read it. I also asked him to decide after reading the presentation whether this was to be our way forward or if he wanted to get out of dentistry and do something he enjoyed, like being a handyman. It really didn't matter to me that we would have to sell the beautiful house we'd built only five years before. But it did matter that whatever he decided, we'd continue to do it as a team: a partnership.

Much to my surprise and delight, Dave said, "Let's go for it. All we can lose is the house, and if I give up on dentistry, we're going to lose that anyway. Oh, and by the way, you missed one of the price references, so I know how much it costs!" Oops! But I knew I'd find the money somehow.

We joined Chris's dental business school, and while Dave concentrated on developing new skills to enable him to provide high-end dentistry, I concentrated on a massive implementation program involving staff training, financial goal setting, and moving Dave's clients to a private dentistry program or sideways onto the list of one of the other two dentists. In fact, we are still legends in Chris's coaching history for our speed of uptake and implementation. We regularly begged him for more input well before the next quarterly workshop.

What's really important to note is that our practice was in the middle of the largest social housing scheme in Inverness. Our clientele was largely unemployed or low-income families, and here we were, moving into private dentistry. We reckoned if we could succeed there, we could succeed anywhere. Another act of madness? No, it was an act of sheer self-belief instilled by Chris!

Meanwhile, I started researching Paddi Lund's story and noticed many parallels between the difficulties he once faced and those Dave was currently experiencing. I saw his philosophy as a way of achieving the life we truly deserved. By the end of December 2001, less than one year after starting our coaching program, we were out of debt, had repaid the loan to my sister, and were planning our next big move: to a purpose-built boutique practice annexed to our house.

At this point, you might think we were truly crazy.

We borrowed money from my dad to build the new practice annexed to our house. We reviewed the files of all 6,500 patients at our Inverness practice and graded them A–D.

The A clients were those who always showed up for their appointments, always paid on time, and were always pleasant with the whole team, not just the dentist.

The Bs were those who generally came into the A category but who had a couple of blips on their record.

The Cs were those who were sometimes okay but often fell short of our expectations.

The Ds were those who we really did not want as clients . . . EVER!

Out of the 6,500, we had only 1,674 A and B-grade clients to whom we sent personal invitations to join us at our new invitation-and-referral-only practice. We sent letters to the rest saying we were closing the practice in Inverness.

The catch? The new practice was fifteen miles away from the Inverness practice, in the middle of a field, four miles from the nearest bus stop! We even invited people to book hay bales in advance if they wanted to come on horseback. Paddi taught us how to create stories that people wanted to tell.

Exactly 572 accepted our invitation. I created a beautiful 'Welcome Book' with loose-leaf pages, which I regularly updated and sent out by snail mail. It was so well-presented that people would bring their copy back to the practice so I could pass it on to someone else. Why? Because they didn't believe a dental practice would send out something so beautiful for them to keep!

Next, I trained my small team to praise all of our clients for being THE BEST, telling them that we only wanted to serve A-grade clients like themselves, and we would reward them handsomely for every new A-grade client they personally referred to us. We sent out gift cards, flowers, tickets to shows, whiskey, wine, and personally engraved silver business card holders with a supply of our cards.

We trained our clients to ring the doorbell on arrival so that we could personally meet and greet them, take their coats, and offer them refreshments. Our bathroom had a range of deodorants, hair products, perfumes, and free toothbrushes and toothpaste. We even had people dragged in by their partners to check out our sparkly toilet seat.

We did not advertise ANYWHERE! We had no external signage, no yellow pages ads, no newspaper ads, and within six months, we had a waiting list of prospective clients. We followed Paddi's lead in creating a happiness-centered business. We had no reception desk and no barriers between our clients and us. I trained my team to become treatment coordinators, providing our clients with a complete range of solutions for their problems. Dave's job was to give his clinical opinion; our job was to present the options and costs and close the deal. And I rewarded my team with a percentage of sales bonuses at the end of each month.

The focus was all on our clients and our team. We built our practice on customer care and network marketing. Our crazy antics paid off, and we earned more money in our last ten years in dentistry than we earned in the previous twenty-five years and had a blast doing it.

The final mention has to go to my third mentor, Tony Gedge of Marketing Pirates of Dentistry, who saw something in me that I hadn't yet discovered. Tony single-handedly brought me to the fore in his business as a writer, speaker, and product creator. But this is another story for another day!

Screw It, We Did It!

BIOGRAPHY

Barb Naisby is a retired dental professional, wife of a golf fanatic, mother to two gorgeous, crazy, grown-up girls, and grandmother to a beautiful granddaughter who is more grown-up than her mum and aunt. She's also been a writer and conference speaker for Tony Gedge's Marketing Pirates of Dentistry and assisted Dr. Paddi Lund at his Happiness Centered Business workshop in London. She somehow found time to help her younger daughter set up the first female-owned and operated chimney sweeping business in Scotland! She now lives in Mexico and is back in business as a network marketer for a worldwide lifestyle company. She spends way too much time on her computer but loves to golf with the wonderful friends she has in San Nicolas de Ibarra.

Connect with Barb Naisby via https://linktr.ee/barbnaisby

CHAPTER 9

THE INNER VOICE

By Carlee Kimball

How can I become so lost? I stared into the mirror at myself, looking at a reflection that I no longer recognized. Who was this person in front of me? On a base level, I knew I was a mom, a wife, a daughter, and a sister. I had been told I was a good worker. I felt like I was a good person, but this reflection wasn't me anymore. The girl I had grown up to be—going through school, graduating high school, and even graduating college—was not the girl I was looking at. This girl—because it certainly wasn't a woman I was looking at—was sad, hurting, and lost. She didn't know where she was going or what path she was on. She was just going through the motions of day-to-day life and not really feeling anything anymore. Staring in the mirror with tears running down my face, my inner voice couldn't help but tell me this was the life I deserved. My inner voice loved telling me that I wasn't deserving of a fulfilling life and that it wasn't going to happen regardless of what I truly wanted.

My inner voice had total control over me at that moment, and looking back, it took control for some time. The inner voice had been telling me for so long that all I was meant to be in this world was a quiet, good girl who does what she's told, and that is all. My inner voice has been telling me these things for years.

I remember, even as a young girl, being told that I couldn't do certain things, being told that my actions were not "ladylike." I remember thinking at first that it wasn't fair. All I wanted to do was sit with my legs crossed on the floor and chase boys around on the playground. But after years of classical conditioning, it became second nature. The obedience had been set in. I stopped questioning, and that little bit of remaining spark dulled so much that I would just go with the flow, regardless of the situation.

By the time I got to high school, I felt like I knew who I was, and I had the confidence to back it up. I was viewed as a leader by my teachers and fellow students, and I felt like one too. I was running the show, quite literally, in the theater department, as well as stepping up with my other extracurricular activities. At that point, I felt completely unstoppable! Little did I know just how small my world was at that point in my senior year of high school.

After high school, I went down the expected path; I got into a local college and earned my associate's degree. I then went to the state university and got my bachelor's degree.

Now, what they don't tell you about that expected path is just how bumpy a road it truly is. After leaving the safety of high school and everything I had known, college was an adventure, to put it nicely. At first, it felt very similar to high school. I mean, of course, the courses were more challenging, and it cost a lot more, but I still held on to that confidence I had, thinking I knew what I was doing. But as the years progressed, everything got harder. In addition to my courses, I was juggling work, school, and personal life. All I could hear was my inner voice telling me that I was going to be a failure, that I wasn't deserving of the degrees for which I was working so hard, and no matter what I did, I was only destined for a mediocre life.

Even on my graduation day from the University, I remember standing in the backroom, waiting to march out with all the other graduates. We all had our caps, gowns, and brand-new hoods, and the excitement filled the air in a loud buzz. I was excited, but to be truthful, I was also relieved to be closing this chapter. Everything I had accomplished should have been something to be happy about. Yet, I still felt like a fraud standing there. My inner voice was telling me that no one cares, even though I had a full section of people who came to sit through a three-hour ceremony just to see me cross the stage.

After college, I continued down the expected path and got a full-time job that would give me the benefits that I logically knew I would need to live my day-to-day life. Now don't get me wrong, I was happy with the choices I had made, and with those, the inner voice quieted down. I knew what I was doing and where I was going and thought this was how it would be.

It wasn't long into my full-time job before I started to notice that I was falling into a pattern. I was finding that even though I was working hard and making good money, I still didn't feel like I had what I needed. I felt like something was missing and that I wasn't getting the fulfillment that I desired. A little bit of a spark was coming back. I tried filling that desire with items such as shoes, purses, and clothes, and I would always justify why I needed the item to make myself feel better.

At this point, I was comfortable, and I was comfortable being comfortable. The desire I previously felt that was coming back had faded again, and I became complacent with my current situation, not yet realizing just how broken I was.

It wasn't until my son got sick that I realized just how lost I had become. That morning started off like any other at the time. My husband had just gotten home from work and was getting our seventeen-month-old up and ready for the day. I was just getting out of bed when my husband came in and told me I needed to call our son's doctor because something was wrong. The weeks up to that point are merely a fog, but that morning put everything back in perspective. I sat in the ER with my son for a good chunk of that day and realized that there was so much more to life than what I had been living.

A few nights later, in the mirror, is where it all had to change. My inner voice was not going to be calling the shots anymore.

I was going to start standing up to myself, for myself. I was going to gain back my confidence and strength. I began repeating some daily affirmations. I am Enough. I am Deserving. I am Strong. I wrote them down and posted them around where I spent most of my time too. I needed them to be forever present to be able to keep the inner voice at bay.

I also started reading or listening to new books focused on personal growth and awakening. I knew that I needed the additional knowledge to help me in the ongoing battle with my inner voice.

I began investing back into myself and my own personal growth. I surrounded myself with other people who had my vision—people who also wanted more and would push me towards bigger and better things.

I was focusing more on myself instead of just the needs of others. One hard lesson I knew I needed to learn was that as hard things were, I could not let what I thought others thought of me affect me anymore. I could not let how other people were feeling affect my mood or my day. I am the only one who can control my day. I was taking charge of my life and focusing on myself, no matter what it meant. Being a mom sometimes means only getting a few minutes to yourself. But even those few minutes of clearing your mind, gathering your clarity, and self-reflection make such the difference every day.

The energy you give off is the energy you're going to get back. Just a way the universe seems to work with me. Making the conscious decision to give more than what I expect created a positive vibe around me. When you put your energy into only the positive items, you will begin to shine even brighter.

As I make these changes in my life, the feeling that I was meant for more has come back to me. These changes haven't been easy, and if I were to let up on any of these items, bad, old habits will begin to creep back in, giving that inner voice the power back.

It sure does feel good to be back to a feeling of clarity and focus that I haven't felt for a very long time. It never occurred to me how big of a role it would play in my life. Knowing that I am meant for more in this world than just the mundane tasks that I have been doing daily is bubbling up my soul.

I needed to check my own mindset to defeat my inner voice, and once I did that, I knew everything would begin to fall in place.

So, if nothing else, I hope that you will try what I've done and see what effect it can have on your own life.

Simply put, the action steps are:

1. Create your own daily affirmations

2. Read something that will support your personal growth

3. Invest in yourself

4. Focus on the positive, great or small

And remember, if you've ever felt like you were meant for more, it is because you are.

BIOGRAPHY

Carlee Kimball is a game-changer. Carlee lives and works in a small rural town in Maine with her son and husband. Although she may be young in years, her mission to help others in concerning their voices reaches beyond her time. She stays motivated, knowing that her work will help others who are going through a tough time.

Connect with Carlee Kimball via https://linktr.ee/CKimball

CHAPTER 10

FROM THE SOIL TO THE STARS

By Charlene C. Wright

December 2020 was supposed to be a great month: my birthday, followed by Christmas, and then New Year. We were putting the year 2020 and the COVID-19 pandemic behind us. But life had other plans.

Rewind to about four years ago. I considered myself healthy. I was a little overweight, but I was okay. My old friend, Vanessa, a coach with an online exercise program, reached out to me (several times) to join her team, and I blew her off; I just wasn't interested. Also, I didn't have the money, I didn't have the time, and I just didn't want to. I always told her, "I'll think about it," but never did. One day, she reached out to me super excited about a new program that was coming out and that I had no choice but to agree. It looked really amazing, so I gave in and joined her team. At the end of the program, I was in the best shape of my life. My legs were toned, my waist was small, my clothes fit, and some were even too big. I even shared my journey on Facebook and Instagram, and I kept this up for years. I received plenty of wonderful feedback, and I felt good I was doing such a great job with it. Of course, I was doing it for myself. I wanted people on my team, but that wasn't really the priority: I just wanted people to see that I was exercising and that they could do it too. Being healthy was my new life, and it was great. I felt good in my skin, my clothes fit, and I was toned; all of that was important to me. This was my life: exercise, work, post about it on social media, go to bed, wake up, and repeat. Wonderful, right? I mean, it was all so easy. Every day was the same, and I just rolled along with it because I knew what was happening.

The COVID-19 pandemic hit the world, and life as we know it turned upside down. Little did I realize that I wasn't working out as I used to, and little by little, I started gaining the weight back. I went to the doctor and got on antidepressants. My father-in-law's health was failing, and he needed a lot more help than my mother-in-law (his primary caregiver) could provide. Unfortunately, there was only so much she could do. So, my husband and I stepped in to do whatever she couldn't. My husband took over, doing everything he could do indoors and out. I helped my mother-in-law do all the tasks that she handled around the house, inside. I started to focus a little more on my health and exercising but not a whole lot. I had to be physically strong to help my husband and care for my father-in-law, but my priority was not me. My priority was the family, and no matter how strong or healthy I felt, I wasn't doing it for me. I was going through the motions because things needed to be done.

Sadly, right after my birthday, my father-in-law passed away, and not long after that, I ended up contracting COVID-19. I had to quarantine myself from everyone in the house. So, I spent two weeks in the camper (yes, I had power). It was actually cold in Florida that December for a change. So, it wasn't awful. However, it was very lonely, and I spent a lot of time outside by the fire pit. I ate and slept a lot. At that time, I was also grieving the loss of my father-in-law and the fact that I was unable to be near the rest of my family. My recovery was compensated by food consumption and sleep. There was nothing in between. I was either sitting at the fire pit eating and napping outside or in the camper, eating and sleeping. It was really boring when I was awake. I couldn't go into the house and be near people. All I had were my thoughts, lots of food, and plenty of sleep.

When my father-in-law passed away, our world stopped. We wondered what we were going to do without him. During my quarantine, I had a lot of time to reflect on my past, think about my present, and wonder about my future. I did not like where I was. I realized I hadn't loved myself all year. I let life get to me and then used it as an excuse to eat, be lazy, and complain about how life was hard. As if I was the only one going through this. I didn't realize how selfish I was being. I was taking my health for granted, the result of which was my weight gain. I was on antidepressants. This was not the life I pictured living. This was not the person I wanted to be. And I definitely did not like having my children seeing me like this. Something had to change. But what?

Something I never really fully noticed until January 2021, something I never understood until then, was how easy it was for life to happen and the weight to "sneak up" on you. It is easy to think you look and feel good, but it hits you another way when you look into the mirror and are not able to recognize the person staring back at you. I was at a new low. I was at the lowest that I had ever been in my life. I was unsure what to think and how to feel. I didn't want to look at my reflection anymore. I mean, I was healthy, right? But did I feel good? And the truth was no. I didn't feel good. I didn't feel good about the way I looked, about my circumstances, and about how I handled them. I needed new clothes for work and ordered everything a size larger because my clothes started to get uncomfortable. Nothing really fitted anymore. And it was in that exact moment of hitting the 'Complete Order' button for $300 worth of new clothing that I realized I really needed to do something. Something had to change. I had to do something for myself. I wasn't healing by being sad. I wasn't healing myself by eating comfort food. I wasn't healing by just digging into my nine-to-five. I essentially gave up and let life control me. I just went through the motions. This simply was not the life I wanted to live. This was not me at all.

The new year started, and I jumped headfirst into my journey for me. I joined a mentoring program. I took a couple of classes to improve my knowledge of fitness and health. I really needed to get back to doing what I loved and sharing my journey. I mean, I shared my journey before. But it wasn't really a journey, it was more of, 'Hey, look at me, I'm exercising!' But this time was different. This time, my journey was a little bit of self-discovery with a little less of 'Hey, look at me.' This was life. This was reality. I was holding myself accountable and dedicated to myself and my health. I decided that I was doing this for me and me alone. I had to go all the way down into the rabbit hole to realize that and to make the decision to really make this journey. I don't ever want to go there again.

It took me forty-seven years to realize this. It took all this time and all this "trauma" for me to be happy with who I am and learn who I really wanted to be. I don't want to be skinny. I just want to be healthy. Becoming strong is a side effect I'll take.

My journey is still full of ups and downs, but it's only just beginning. I'm thankful to have a handful of supportive people on my side. And I will forever be grateful to them for pushing me to be the best me I can be.

You should not throw in the towel when things get hard. That's when you should focus. Don't let bad situations handle you. Think about *what* is going on. Think about *why* it is going on and why you feel the way you do. Then, you handle it.

Setbacks are part of life. But how we handle them makes us who we are.

BIOGRAPHY

Charlene C. Wright is currently studying to be a National Academy of Sports Medicine, Nutrition and Fitness coach. Her love for fitness and health began easily enough, but her ideas of fitness and health changed along the way. She discovered a passion and desire to help others to become healthy. With her vivacious spirit and talkative nature, her journey began. Charlene loves camping, kayaking, mountain biking, and anything outdoors. She loves spending time with her husband, Jason, her children, Cassandra and Myles, and her dogs, Cooper and Finn.

Connect with Charlene C. Wright via
https://linktr.ee/IMCCFITNESS

CHAPTER 11

DON'T LET THE NEGATIVES DEVELOP

By Cindy Buxton

Yep, you guessed it . . . I'm a photographer. Over forty years ago, I was told I couldn't do something, and I set out to prove them wrong.

Growing up in rural Nebraska, I was a very shy child, usually hiding behind my parents' legs or a nearby sibling—a man for whom my dad custom-fed cattle asked if I ever talked. I loved when he came to visit but never spoke a word to him. Truth be told, I was very chatty . . . just not around people I didn't know.

I really have very few happy memories from my childhood. Our house was full of tension. My dad was full of bitterness from things that happened to him in the past; he just couldn't let go. If he was miserable, everyone was going to be miserable—and we were. I had multiple stomach ulcers and took 'nerve pills' for years. What hurt most was when my friends would say how great my dad was. He was—when we were out hunting. I always longed for him to be like that at home.

We went to a little country church that had this incredible pipe organ. The entire congregation, young and old, sang at the top of their lungs. Our Christmas programs were amazing. We also attended school there and left towards the end of my third-grade year, the day after my closest sister was confirmed. The teacher would say I didn't turn in my homework and deprive me of my lunch. She didn't like taking extra time to teach just one third-grader, so she would teach me alongside the fourth-grade boys, who were all much older than me. It was best to get me out of there. Town school was a big adjustment. The teacher was an old crab, we had hot lunch, and Roy had the coolest colored pens. I was already writing in cursive, so I was a bit bored. I passed the time staring at the alphabet above the blackboard and memorized it backwards. Surprisingly, that 'skill' would come in handy a couple of times later in life.

The first crushing blow to any confidence I had gained was stripped away in the fourth grade—the day our music teacher told me I was a monotone. To this very day, you can sit right next to me and not hear me sing. *Never* tell someone they can't do something! I know his words held me back for years. Be careful of what you speak. Life and death are in the power of the tongue.

On my eleventh birthday, I purchased a 110 camera at the drugstore. In high school, I took pictures for the yearbook, and two local papers would hire me to cover games and events. This was the beginning of my love of photography.

There were only twenty-four in my high school class, but I would not give the Salutatorian speech at our graduation. My friend Jackie stepped up to do so, and to this day, it's one of the many reasons I like her so much. This farm girl chose to skip college and attend photography school in Minneapolis. My oldest sister cried on the way home after moving me to a furnished apartment near the school. Our first assignment was to photograph people in our neighborhood, and we had to ask them to sign a release—the first big step out of my comfort zone. I met some pretty 'interesting' characters. After that assignment, our instructor asked the locals in my class to help me find a new place to live. I think back on those days, listening to the neighbors arguing . . . maybe it felt like home. Those first few weeks were interesting. The day I found my white car covered with blood was the day I decided to move.

Meanwhile, back home in a neighboring town, the local florist was starting a photography business. My cousin was a florist there and told her I would never be able to shoot a wedding because I was way too shy. The girl she knew would have been, but a completely different person moved back to Nebraska. Yes, I could shoot a wedding, and I was very good at it. I worked there for fifteen months, and with the encouragement of my friend, KC, I walked out the door into a life of entrepreneurship shortly before my twentieth birthday. Besides a few bartending gigs to help pay the bills in my early years, I never had a boss ever again!

The photography business almost never happened. I needed a $10,000 loan to purchase two backdrops, two stools, three studio lights, and another camera for my studio. I was only nineteen, and the banker wouldn't let my dad co-sign the loan. I went to my grandfather. At first, he was hesitant. I think he saw the passion I had, and when I said if he helped me get started by co-signing for me, I vowed to take care of my mom for the rest of my life. That's all it took to convince him. Until now, I kept his secret that he did this for me. He had twenty-five grandchildren and couldn't help them all in this way. But he knew I was serious about helping my mom get out of an abusive marriage.

For the first year, I had an office in my parent's sunroom, and my photo studio was in the basement. One couple's engagement photos were taken in our grove behind the machine shed, right next to our pet burial grounds. Who knew meeting them through my photography business in my early days would later come full circle?

When my parents finally divorced, mom built a small home with a full basement for my photography business. I made her the same promise I made to my grandpa. A few years later, God brought my soulmate into my life. It was mom's idea for him to move in. He was on the road all week and at our house on weekends. I would pat Faron on the head like a puppy and say, "Can I keep him, momma?" I still occasionally do that, and he still tolerates it.

Every year, the photography business grew, soon outgrowing our little house. Building our dream home/studio started to become a reality. Our intention was to design the studio I needed and put a house on top. Mom had remarried and lost her husband a week before their first anniversary, so bringing her back home with us became part of the plan. We spent many hours creating a grand outdoor studio, and business flourished. Three years later, we made another huge investment and converted to a totally digital studio. Doing so at the time put us in the forefront. That same technology would later contribute to our demise. Photography isn't the profession it once was; the times are just changing. Now, people would rather go out to the pasture or the city streets instead of the traditional studio. That's okay with me. My main focus after forty years is business portraiture. Pun intended. I got out of the wedding biz in 2012. I had captured memories for more than a thousand couples. Every single day, I can wish many of 'my couples' a happy anniversary on Facebook. Today, I still shoot a few families and seniors, but my new love is network marketing. God seems to place what you need, just when you need it.

Change . . . it's the only thing you can really count on. Months change, seasons change, life changes. Life is a continuous rollercoaster. Many changes came into our lives, but the last ninety-five days of 2015 were a gut punch. At the end of September, my dad passed away. It wasn't unexpected; he was in the nursing home for nine years. As tumultuous as my childhood was, we had come to an understanding and had a great relationship as adults. Faron played a big role in that. Even if it took dementia for him to say, "I love you," I knew he was proud of me.

The following month, one of the consultants on my team was killed in a car accident. A twenty-seven-year-old father of two young children. He was so full of life and ambition. I often wonder how far he would have gone.

Two weeks later, my accountant of thirty-four years was also killed in a car accident. He was quite the character but was like a big brother to me. This was a huge blow but so surreal. He and his wife had just gotten out of their wheelchairs from a near-fatal accident five months earlier. His wheelchair sat eerily empty in the middle of the room when I went to visit his wife, and she was back in hers. With so many other changes going on in our lives, I just felt lost.

Throughout all this, Mom and I talked about these deaths a lot, especially my dad. Even after all he put her through, even almost strangling her once, I think all she ever wanted was to be loved. That still breaks my heart.

Three other deaths affected me more than usual during this time. After one of those funerals, I said, "What else could possibly happen?" Remember how I said, 'Watch your words?' On December 21, a friend's son was killed in Afghanistan. With him being a New York City police officer, it was quite an ordeal. Mom and I talked so much about this—how awful it was that it happened just before Christmas. Never in a million years would I have guessed Mom would be gone by the end of the week. She literally dropped dead walking into my sister's house for our Christmas dinner. I guess I fulfilled my promise that I'd always take care of my mom and never put her in a nursing home, but this wasn't how I pictured it. I thank God every day for bringing Faron into my life. Not many men would live in the same house as their mother-in-law for twenty-seven years. Not once do I ever remember him being anything but loving towards her. That's the kind of man every woman needs to look for.

As we were trying to find a new normal over the next few months, I was given the opportunity to attend a Tony Robbins event . . . a lifelong dream of mine. I became a Firewalker! Another feat I never saw myself accomplishing. After stepping on a bumblebee while barefoot when I was five, I rarely went barefoot, even indoors. I certainly never expected to kick off my shoes and socks and walk across hot coals! You can do anything with the right mindset.

So many times, life has tried to beat me down. I could have easily given up, but I chose not to. That's the one thing we can control: how we react to things. Guard your mindset with all you've got. Sometimes, it's those closest to you who'll try to talk you out of following your dreams. Many times, it's because they themselves fear change, and they don't want you to succeed without them.

What if my dream was to sing? Those few words out of my teacher's mouth could have crushed my lifelong ambition. I will never speak death over anyone's dreams, no matter how big they are. What if my grandpa didn't believe in me? Where would I be today?

Life happens, don't let the negatives develop; stay positive. Our latest curveball was Faron waking up for work with his hand not working properly; he had a mild stroke. We also found out that he has had more than ten prior silent strokes. This wouldn't be that catastrophic, except that he's a truck driver and the DOT won't let him renew his CDL for at least one year. We were not prepared to hear this, but once again, we were grateful it wasn't worse. With him off work for a year, our plans were once again derailed! We just had to re-adjust the sails and keep moving forward through life. Together, there isn't anything we can't do!

Don't let anyone say you can't do anything: prove you can. From time to time, things will come out of nowhere and try to knock you down. Sometimes, they come in droves. This Spring, I suddenly lost my business partner. Jim and Joanie were the couple I photographed in my parents' grove. Funny how three decades later, we united with a passion for helping others live life to the fullest. I'm determined to fulfill the legacy she left behind.

It's okay to take time to grieve but don't set up residency there. Continue to live and enjoy each day God grants you. Most of all, BELIEVE IN YOURSELF, and live life with no regrets!

BIOGRAPHY

Cindy Buxton has been self-employed since she was nineteen years old. A hard-working Nebraska farm girl who didn't have any desire to go to college, she chose to move to Minneapolis and attend photography school. After working for a studio for a little over a year, she stepped into the world of entrepreneurship. She enjoyed decades of capturing her clients' special memories and making people smile. As the world changed with the development of technology, so did the photography profession. Her perseverance led her into a new career in network marketing. Cindy worked her way to the Leadership Council with her first company. Her passion for helping people is fulfilled every day by helping her teammates overcome obstacles and work hard to create the life of their dreams. Cindy married her husband Faron in 1989, and they continue to live in northeast Nebraska.

Connect with Cindy Buxton via https://linktr.ee/cindybuxton

CHAPTER 12

TOUCHING HEARTS AND CHANGING LIVES

By Jacalyn Price

Overcoming Challenges and Becoming Unstoppable

My name is Jacalyn Price. I see, hear, feel, and know that my purpose in life is to touch hearts and change lives, one person at a time.

This is my story.

Growing up, I was the oldest of seven children. This meant that I took on the role of 'Carer.' I helped both my mother and father. Mom had problems with every pregnancy, especially the last two. My father was a hard worker. He worked in rutile and zircon mines.

I was very close to my grandparents, and I loved to visit their house often. Grandma loved her craft, so much so that she passed it down to my mother. They were both very talented. My grandfather loved working with wood. Even cancer didn't stop him. When he was sick, he made tables out of small pieces of coloured wood, which he cut up. Every table was made of a different pattern. I consider myself extremely lucky to have one of his tables.

Fast forward to when I was eighteen. I wanted to join the police force and work in the forensics department. However, I didn't meet the qualifications they had for a female back in the day: twenty-four years old and 5'6". Even though I was neither, I kept my fitness levels high by running and swimming. When I was thirty-two, the height limit for the forensics department was dropped. Given this change, I tried my luck again. However, this time, I was too old: thirty-two years old.

So, I decided to pursue a career in pathology, for which I attended a technical college. I worked at the Royal Newcastle Hospital, working one of the shifts. The hospital had a view of the ocean. I found it relaxing listening to the waves at night, after which I'd go for a short run to the baths. It was all great exercise.

On December 28, 1989, an earthquake hit Newcastle. The hospital was damaged. We were relocated to the John Hunter Hospital as soon as its construction was completed. The land on which Royal Newcastle Hospital was once located is now filled with motels and units. Call it a developer's dream.

Changing Your Name . . . Changing How You Live and Feel

I was not happy with the name given to me. Why? It didn't *feel* like me. At the age of twenty-one, I decided to change my name with the help of my aunt, Eve, who was one of my mentors. I chose a new name and a new spelling: Jacalyn. I still kept my original name; I used it as my second name. I did not realize it at the time, but my aunt was using her second name. Also, my grandfather changed his surname when he travelled from England to Australia in 1921 (this journey took six weeks).

Now, looking back at my life, I've always taken the role of carer; I still hold this role, taking care of my ninety-year-old dad. I was a carer for my mother as well, but we lost her to a severe stroke in August 2019.

I held a designation and worked in a place where you had to provide solutions to people. I worked as a pathology technician for over twenty-five years. I also worked in blood transfusion and haematology and as an assistant in diagnosing health and disease.

A Simple Fall at Work

One day, my entire work dynamic changed. I had a simple fall at work. Little did I know what this had in store for me. The fall led to me suffering from intense pain, and after a short period of time, I lost the use of my left leg. How could a simple fall have done that? I was diagnosed with Reflex Sympathetic Dystrophy. I was put under the care of a rehabilitation specialist and a neurologist and placed in pain management clinics.

Thirteen years later, and after much work in rehab at the Toronto Private Hospital, I regained the use of my left leg. I had to do hydrotherapy and physiotherapy three times a week. I needed nerve blocks in my left hip, Guanethidine blocks in my left foot, and ketamine infusions for pain relief. I was unable to drive, and I required help at home for basic necessities.

Let me tell you: nerve pain is one of the most intense pains you can have. I was under a lot of medication to keep it under control. I could not stand anyone or anything touching my left leg. The pain clinics taught me many to keep the pain under control, namely meditation and deep breathing.

My advice is this: Never let pain control you. Your mindset is the key—your subconscious mind.

What You Think You Become

I spent thirteen years between a wheelchair, walking frame, and crutches. When I tried to get back to work, I was told, "You are too old," and "You have been out of work too long." I began looking for other ways to work. I did some business courses and had a business coach. This led me on a trip to Thailand, where we had a wonderful experience. The monks blessed us, and we lit lanterns and released them into the sky. Imagine all those lanterns floating skyward—picture perfect.

I continued my studies, learning, and teaching, as Jim Rohn would say. I was an Avon sales leader for seven years. My mother and Aunt Eve would assist me with getting orders ready. Aunt Eve also helped with the delivery. Having this new job allowed me to meet and bond with many people. Sometimes, people (especially lonely ladies) just needed a person to listen to and share their problems. I advised wherever I could. As they say, a problem shared is a problem halved. I became one of the top fifty sales leaders in Australia.

Tony Robbins: My Next Adventure

My next adventure was with Tony Robbins. I am a Firewalker! I am unstoppable!

Before I did the Firewalk experience, I spoke to my Aunt Eve about it. This was back in August 2018. Aunt Eve was ill and suffering from breathing problems. She asked me if I was going to do the Firewalk experience. I replied, "Of course, I am," not knowing back then how I would pull it off. Aunt Eve passed away the following month.

I kept my promise to her. I walked the Firewalk that September. Tony Robbins prepares you for it and makes you feel that you are walking across cool moss. I felt that my Aunt Eve was waiting for me on the other side.

The Power of the Subconscious Mind

On November 29, 2018, I was hit by a taxi when walking on a pedestrian crossing. The hit took me airborne, during which I did not know what would happen next. I was lucky enough to be pushed to the other side, and luckily not in the front. Otherwise, I would have been run over. My Aunt Eve was looking after me.

I recall hitting the road on my side and watching the taxi wheels go past me . . . very close! I sat up and was unable to move my right arm. Everyone came running. My old judo days must have helped me out as I did a break fall. I shattered my arm, and it broke in six places. I was taken to the hospital by ambulance. My mum, dad, and other family members came to visit me there.

I was in a great deal of pain, for which I took morphine. I loved the green whistle. I had an operation the following day. It took six hours to put my arm back together. I was covered in bruises, and my arm was multi-coloured. I spent four and a half months in the hospital.

My first operation involved getting pins and plates in my shoulder and wrist and wires and screws in my elbow. In July 2019, I needed a complete elbow replacement. I needed help at home, seven days a week. I had to do physiotherapy and hydrotherapy. I also got a counsellor. During that time, I learned about the power of Chakra, using breathing techniques for it, meditation, yoga, exercises, and tapping the power of the subconscious mind. Now, I don't need any pain relief medication other than Panadol. I have lost 25 percent of the use of my arm. But that does not stop me.

My Mother's Stroke

In June 2019, my mother suffered from a stroke. I was at home during the time, recovering from my surgeries; I was unable to drive. My mother had woken up at 3 a.m. and needed to go to the bathroom. She couldn't walk, so she had to crawl there and back. She phoned me at 6:30 a.m. and told me that she was not feeling well. I asked her if she needed an ambulance, to which she said yes. I called for one and rang my brother, Graham, to let him know so he could pick me up. The ambulance got there before we could.

My mother had suffered from a severe stroke. Her left leg went numb, she had trouble talking, and she had weakness in one of her arms. We got three ambulances and took her to John Hunter Hospital. We had to move her furniture and put her on a portable stroller.

After the stroke, my mother was unable to swallow and had to be tube-fed. She had to spend ten weeks at the hospital. She began to get feeling back in her leg, and so began the rehab. During those ten weeks, I had an operation on my elbow. I would be picked up from the hospital at Mainland Private, pick dad up, and then visit mum. I'd do the reverse when coming back.

My mother struggled and fought as hard as she could, but she succumbed to pneumonia many times. We lost her in August. We all miss her so much, especially my dad. They were married for sixty-seven years. She was the love of his life. Mum loved to cook, loved her craft, always sewing, knitting, and crocheting for children, grandchildren, and great-grandchildren. She taught us to love and be loved.

Networking Groups

I joined networking groups and learned that the people you mix with make a difference in your life. In my Bx Business Networking Group, I applied for the Business Awards. I made the final cut and won! Business of the Year in Business Services 2020! I have the honour and privilege of having an article in Bx xClusive Magazine. This boosted my confidence and business to another level.

I am now in other networking groups. We have businesses supporting each other in the Maitland Business Chamber. I work with like-minded people: this has become my mission in life.

Initially, my original goal for getting into business was to help mum and dad more. But I had other motivations. My sister, Jen, was diagnosed with breast cancer. The radiation treatment cost $10,000. She had to borrow money to pay for it. My Coach has Stage 4 Melanoma, the two-year treatment for which costs $110,000 per year. After I shared this with my coach, I decided that there had to be a better way to go about this.

How many more people will I be able to help with the help of my networking business? My mission is to set up a foundation for people with illnesses to access funds for medication and treatment. I want to be able to take the burden off families.

Touching hearts and changing lives—that's my motto. Live your dreams!

> "Some people come into our lives and leave footprints
> on our hearts and we are never ever the same."[2]

—Flavia Weedn

Finding your 'Why' is like having a lighthouse that guides you toward fulfilment. Change your story; change your life. If I can do it, so can you.

Have it in you to overcome any challenge you come across and become stronger for it.

BIOGRAPHY

Jacalyn Price won Business of the Year in Business Services in 2020. She has an article published in Bx xClusive Magazine. She belongs to the following network marketing groups: Bx Business

---

2   "Flavia Weedn Quotes (Author of Flavia and the Dream Maker)," Goodreads (Goodreads), accessed October 6, 2021, https://www.goodreads.com/author/quotes/179541.Flavia_Weedn.

Network Marketing Group, Port Stephens Women in Business, Lake Macquarie Women in Business, Maitland Business Chamber, Your Business Connections Group, and Happy Neighborhood Project Group. She has been the host and speaker at her business networking events. Her key to success is personal development. Some of her biggest influences are Bob Proctor, Mary Morrissey, Jim Rohn, Tony Robbins, Grant Cardone, Simon Sinek, and Zig Ziglar, to name a few. Her life's mission is to set up a foundation for people with illnesses to access funds for treatment and medication. This was after her sister, Jen, was diagnosed with breast cancer and had to pay a large sum for radiation. Jacalyn loves taking burdens off families, touching hearts, changing lives. Every day for her is a new day with new thoughts, strengths, and possibilities.

Connect with Jacalyn Price via https://linktr.ee/JacalynP

CHAPTER 13

KEEP YOUR EYE ON THE PRIZE

By Jacqueline B. Harrington

I grew up with various relatives, but there was one with whom I lived the longest: my aunt Beulah. She always told me that I could be whatever I wanted to be, and I believed her. So, when I experienced a meteoric rise in the airline industry after eighteen months, I was happy, but I did not think it extraordinary. For the next ten years, I enjoyed my job in organisational development and travelled wherever my company operated, but I always knew I wanted to run my own successful business. I took a correspondence course in fashion merchandising because I wanted my very own dress shop. Then I pursued my associate's degree in business management. However, with the failure of my marriage after eleven years, I had to turn all of my attention to supporting my two sons. There would be no time to study because of working full time and taking care of the boys.

When I was asked to lead the first airport automation project, I took on that task with everything I had. The project was a resounding success, and as a reward, I was promoted to manage user support throughout the network. The dream of having my own business never left me. So, by this time, I had opened a custom clothing store in a very nice part of the city—just on the outskirts—and I had a lovely up-market clientele. The store was successful from day one. So now I had my own home, car, and my kids were attending private school. Because I travelled so much, I had a live-in helper, and I had my custom sewing shop, which would become a well-known establishment by the time I was ready to retire. I even took my kids to London on vacation. Life was good. I was on top of the world.

When I was called into the director's office and told that I was being retrenched, I went numb. My world froze. I didn't see it coming. My manager explained that he had made a mistake with the paperwork and was sorting things out. He said that I would be back at my desk within two weeks. Those two weeks became two years. I lost everything. My business was not making enough money to take care of itself, my mortgage, car payments, kids' school fees, my helper . . . you get the idea. I couldn't find a job, so I moved back home with my aunt. I felt like a failure. What happened to my life? I decided I would go abroad and work for a while as a babysitter or housekeeper just to get some money together to pay a few bills. So, I left my kids and my business with a friend who offered to help, and off I went. Yep, a drowning man would grasp at a straw. I sent money home as fast as I made it. During the five months I was away, my kids were not well treated. They didn't tell me. My friend spent my money and dropped my two sons (aged twelve and fourteen) off at their dad's house late one night. He stopped sending them to school. Someone called me and filled me in on what was happening, and I immediately returned home.

Now, I had nothing. In my ignorance, I even lost my house to the bank. I was thirty-five years old with two kids, no job, no financial support, and no business. My friend had run the business to the ground, and I met my former husband (who had

NOTHING to do with the business), conducting a closing down sale to get paid for having the kids for five weeks.

What could I do at this point? Move back in with my aunt, take my kids to Australia undocumented, take my kids to California undocumented, or marry a friend who had been asking me for some time? The first three options came with their own set of challenges. I married my friend. In two weeks, I knew I made a grave mistake. He was a terrible husband, and he did not show much interest in my children. It's incredible how you don't see these things until it's too late. But I was determined to make the best of it for the sake of my children and to honour my vows before God. I didn't want to fail at marriage a second time. I stayed for twenty years all up (silly me), but that's for another story.

Around the time that I remarried, I became a financial advisor with a large insurance company. I began to thrive very early. My name was high on the leaderboard with my picture on the wall, and my clientele was growing. But I had become timid in spirit. I couldn't risk the fluctuating income while I was raising two sons. Even though I was married, my husband made it clear that my children were my responsibility and that they had a father. This was from this nice guy who had been my good friend for three years and who knew I received no financial support from my ex-husband. I thought I knew him. I was on my own. I took care of all repairs (working toilets, running water, furnishings, appliances) so that my children could be fairly comfortable. When my husband was unemployed for ten months, I took care of him too. "Be a good Christian," I told myself. "Do it unto God."

So, when the airline offered me a temporary contract after two years of being away, I grabbed it with both hands. This was financial stability. I had spent thirteen and a half years with the airline. I was going home.

Within seven years, I became the organisation's loyalty marketing expert, and I was managing the department. My days were long, and I loved what I did, but I always remembered that they had the power to change my world at any time. Once more, I began to dream of having my own successful business. My kids were now grown and out of the house, so here was my chance. I requested leave without pay to start a loyalty marketing company. They refused to approve it, so I quit. I had the expertise and the financing, and I recalled my aunt saying, "You can be whatever you want." My confidence was revived. I was all in.

The business started out very well. I contracted with the largest mall chain in the country and a few of the hotels. Soon, I began having difficulty collecting payments from the partners. If I sued, who else would partner with me? Needless to say, the venture was an abysmal failure. I was now so deep in debt that I had no idea how I would ever climb out. Later, I was told that all that I was missing was a well-known name on my board of directors.

No business. No job. No money. Deep in debt. Whenever I heard a noise at my gate, I would peep to see if it was the landlord because I didn't have the rent. I hardly had any food. Early in the mornings, I would take my shopping bag to the vacant lot down the street and collect the mangoes that had fallen to the ground. I would take them home, wash and dry them, and fill my fruit basket. Sometimes, I would buy one ounce of cheese at the corner shop or one or two eggs, and that would be my protein. I took my last $100 and started a food business, but I needed more money to pay my bills. I was careful not to use the car too much because I didn't have money for petrol. I felt like walking, and walking . . . and walking off the edge of the earth.

One day, in despair, I told God I would not move until He told me what I should do. As I lay on the couch, waiting, I remembered an employment agency that was owned by an ex-colleague. This was a Tuesday evening. I called them on Wednesday, and they told me to come in right away. I went in on Thursday, and on Friday morning, I was working in administration for an international oil company. Thank You, God!! On my second day on the job, my bank kept calling me to discuss my arrears, and the call kept cutting out. I kept taking the call because they were that close to repossessing my car, and I had to talk to them that day, to buy me some time now that I was working. I succeeded in persuading the bank to wait, but I lost the job. The supervisor found I had too many personal phone calls.

The agency took my word that this was not my usual way of operating and found me another job, and then another until I found a permanent job. In the next five years, I completed my bachelor's (with first-class honours) and master's in science degree, and my food business grew. I was now supplying the largest grocery chain in the country but on a very small scale. When the government changed and contracts were not renewed, I did not want to be out of a job again, and I had become too timid to rely on my small business to sustain me. By this time, I had my temporary resident visa for Australia, and this is how I left my home in Trinidad and Tobago and migrated to Australia.

At the age of fifty-three, I arrived in Australia with five suitcases, a prayer, and two months' worth of survival money. Within five years, I repaid my debts, and I had moved into my own home, (partly owned by the bank, of course). During this time, I kept looking for the right business opportunity. I had decided that I would remain at mid-level in the corporate world so as not to have too much responsibility when I started my business. But when I was constantly encouraged to apply for higher positions, I took my eye off the prize and abandoned my plan. I landed this fantastic job in another organisation with a salary just shy of six figures. But the cost was high. The commute was two hours each way, and it was a terrible fit. I lasted three months. When I got the letter, I didn't read it. I simply packed up under the watchful eye of the manager, and I left. I remember talking to myself on the way out and saying, "I choose JOY. I choose JOY." I went home, indulged in a short pity party, and started sending out job applications.

Contrary to what many say, 2020 was a very good year for me. At the beginning of 2020, I was successful with application #71. In July 2020, in the middle of the COVID-19 pandemic, my girlfriend introduced me to a business opportunity that ticked all the boxes for me. It was what I had been looking for, and I embraced it wholeheartedly.

Now, one year later, I feel the past year has been nothing short of tremendous. I have undergone much transformation and development. I found out that if my dream is high, it is not enough to believe I can do it, although that is an essential component. But I also have to climb towards it. For the past year, I have set my eyes firmly on the prize, and I have been engaging in activities that are taking me closer to my dream. It was when I engaged in these activities that I met Matt Morris. I have learnt that if you keep your eye on the prize, no matter what happens, no matter how much life steers you away from your desire, you will find your way and achieve what you want. I still have my dream, but it has now evolved. It's not just about me being successful anymore but also about how I can positively impact the lives of millions in the process.

My aunt is gone now, but her words continue to encourage me. My dream is happening. No matter what, you can be whatever you want to be if you keep your eye on the prize.

BIOGRAPHY

Jacqueline B. Harrington is a 'Health in Wealth' promoter, direct sales entrepreneur, blogger, and author. Jacquie has built several businesses in the past and uses her more than twenty years of experience to focus on online marketing and providing the missing link in self-care. Utilising the skills she developed while earning her master's degree in maritime management, Jacquie researches proactive health maintenance and creates empowering blogs and videos on supporting wellness to live better, longer. She also holds a bachelor's degree in social policy, which supports her sensitivity to social needs. She continues to contribute to the lives of the underprivileged and is committed to making a positive impact on those around her by encouraging them to pursue their best lives. Born in Trinidad and Tobago, Jacquie now resides in Melbourne, Australia. She is a proud mom of two and a beaming grandmother of four. She loves to sing jazz and gospel.

Connect with Jacqueline B. Harrington via
https://linktr.ee/jacquiebharrington

CHAPTER 14

LIFE LESSONS LEARNED

By Jana Ratkovich

Growing up as a kid in the mid-to-late 60s and early 70s, with my siblings, in St. Louis Park, MN, was great. We would play outside all day with the neighborhood kids, riding bikes, making forts, climbing trees, playing games, and going to the school playground across the street. We just used our imaginations and had so much fun and freedom. We just had to be home in time for dinner. As a kid, when I thought about what I wanted to be when I grew up, I wanted to be a stay-at-home mom like my mom.

Fast forward about twenty-some years, my wish of becoming a mom came true. But instead of being a stay-at-home mom, I became a single working mom. When I was twenty-six, I became pregnant. When I found out, I had already broken up with the father. I went to the doctor to confirm my suspicions of being pregnant, and I was right: I was pregnant. The nurse practitioner said that this was a lot to do on my own and that there were other options. I burst into tears. There was no way I was going to have an abortion, especially after what my mom went through, losing three full-term babies before having me taken out six weeks early so I wouldn't die in the last trimester. No way! That was never an option. What if this was my only chance of having a kid. I always wanted kids since I was little. I would figure it out. I was going to have this baby. It was the best decision of my life!! It wasn't easy, but I had so much support from my family and friends over the years raising him. It helped me become a strong independent woman.

Looking back at my life, I think the first place I was a leader was out on the softball field. When catching or pitching, I would call out the next move on the field based on how many outs, strikes, balls, and the placement of people on the bases. It didn't scare me because I didn't even realize I was being a leader; I was just playing the game and helping my team play our best.

As for social situations, I was a quiet and shy kid, not very good at meeting new people. I would stand back or stay near my mom or my older sister, who was more social. To give an idea of how shy I was, my mom once told me a story of my Sunday school teacher asking my mom if I ever talked. I was three or four at the time. I was too shy just to go up and talk to someone, especially if I didn't know them. Instead, I preferred to let people come to me. I was definitely not as outgoing as my dad, who could strike up a conversation with any stranger. But just because those of us on the quieter side don't like being in the spotlight, it doesn't mean we aren't smart, fun to be around, or don't have anything to say. We just aren't as self-confident to speak up, or maybe it's because others won't let us get a word in edgewise.

As I said, when I was a kid, I didn't speak up much, especially in school, unless I knew for sure I had the correct answer. But when I would go for a walk with just my dad, he said I would talk his ear off, and he couldn't get a word in. So, that means we do have something to say; we just have to feel comfortable around someone before doing so.

As an adult, I have been working to overcome this shyness, stepping out of my comfort zone, and becoming more like dad, being comfortable talking to everyone. I want to break through the barriers holding me back from becoming a great and respected leader. I believe that the world needs more leaders who lead by example and who are honest, hard-working, humble, kind, respectful of others, have integrity, and are passionate about creating other leaders. I believe a great leader creates other leaders by encouraging and teaching them to become their best selves, not by holding them back. You will shine more by helping others—even if they rise above you—than you would by holding them back and trying to stay on top. I have learned it is far better not to be jealous of others' lives and successes. Instead, help them celebrate those successes. Believe me, I know all too well how easy it is to look at others' lives and become jealous of the things they have that you want but don't have. If they have what you want, ask them to help you achieve it for yourself. The more you help others, the happier and more blessed you will be. So, when you see someone who is shy, give them encouragement and positive feedback. It will provide them with the confidence to grow. Just because we are shy doesn't mean we don't have greatness within us. Sometimes, all we need is just a little nudge or the right person to believe in us, to give us the confidence to prove to ourselves that we have what it takes and to push us out of our comfort zone and help us become the best version of ourselves.

We often have more potential than we are afraid to admit, and others around us see that potential before we do. When I was in my early twenties, living in San Diego, I had a wonderful boss who saw my leadership skills before I did and offered me a promotion to become supervisor over five data processors at our company. She had so much confidence in me—definitely more than I had in myself—that she told me I should just try it out, and if I didn't feel like it was a fit, then I could go back to my previous position. She knew I could do it but needed to nudge me past my lack of self-confidence. I took the job and kept it. It was a great experience that led me to further promotions.

I think this is God's way of nudging us in the direction He wants us to go to fulfill our purpose and be at the right place at the right time to help others on their journey as well. Everyone has their own unique journey in this life, but they all intertwine at the right time to help each other continue to grow and fulfill our destiny. Have you ever had someone come into your life and help you through something you were going through, and then all of a sudden, you realize that you drifted apart and never saw them again? I have—more than once. I definitely believe that certain people cross our paths for a reason, and sometimes, it is just for a season: to help us in a particular situation and then move on. And then, some enter our life and stay for the long run. I have many of these angels who have been a blessing in my life throughout the years. Thank you to all of you for helping me on my life's journey and helping me break through the barriers that were holding me back from being a great leader. I believe that being a great leader will better equip me to continue following my passion for helping others.

Below is a list of some of the other things that I have learned along my journey.

1. Never stop learning; you are never too young or old to learn something new.

2. Read the Bible.

3. Have faith in God and yourself; you are stronger than you think and can do so much more than you realize.

4. There is always something to be thankful for in good times and bad.

5. Work hard, do your best, and always do the right thing even when no one is watching.

6. Spend as much time with your loved ones as you can; you never know how much time anyone has left.

7. Be a good listener.

8. Always be kind and generous.

9. Do little things that make people feel special.

10. Compliment everyone.

11. Always tell the truth; it will be less painful in the long run than telling one lie after another to hide the truth because the truth always comes out.

12. Engage in positive thinking. You are what you say you are, so say positive, uplifting things about yourself every day! Bless yourself! You will love the results!

13. SMILE! It is contagious.

14. Faith over fear—this helped me so much throughout the past year.

Christian radio has become a significant influence in my life and has really helped me through the ups and downs of life with songs that reflect exactly what I need to hear at any given moment. It has also helped me not get as angry at other people's bad driving.

Currently, my favorite song is by MercyMe, "Say I Won't," especially this part:

> ". . . I can do all things
> Through Christ who gives me strength
> So keep on saying I won't
> And I'll keep proving you wrong

I'm gonna run
No I'm gonna fly
I'm gonna know what it means to live
And not just be alive . . ."[3]

BIOGRAPHY

Jana Ratkovich, who was born and raised in Minnesota, went from being a shy kid to a hard-working, dedicated single mom to becoming a published author. She has a passion for helping others and is always willing to lend a helping hand. She loves traveling, being out in nature and seeing wildlife, walking, hiking, and her new favorite, kayaking, especially in the fall. Her mission is to inspire others to become their best selves by stepping out of their comfort zone. If she can do it, so can you.

Connect with Jana Ratkovich via https://linktr.ee/Jana_Ratkovich

---

3   "MercyMe - Say I Won't Lyrics," musiXmatch, accessed August 26, 2021, https://www.musixmatch.com/lyrics/MercyMe/Say-I-Won-t.

CHAPTER 15

EVERYTHING IS FIGURE-OUT-ABLE

By Jared Crebs

Before entering the business world, I had just graduated from college as a music teacher. I was sinking in a pool of credit card and student loan debt. I was living paycheck to paycheck, and I was unsure if I could support a family. I was twenty-six years old, living in the ghetto of Denton, Texas, in a little yellow house from the fifties with a dirt driveway.

I had a car with no air-conditioning and 200,000 miles on it. It was a red 1992 Pontiac Grand Am with a big dent in the front. I remember constantly worrying about my car breaking down. I needed an online business because my financial situation was not going to improve with my job. My plan was to succeed or die trying. I had no business skills, but I had the *only* three things that mattered for success: I was willing, coachable, and hungry.

It took me about two years to replace my job income. I have now been full time with my online business for over thirteen years. I'm happily married, and my wife has been able to quit her job and join me in our business. She has freedom too! We have a blast together. Our online business takes care of all our needs and much more. My student loans and credit card debts are completely paid off. We live in a nice part of town in San Antonio, Texas. We are able to save, invest, give back, create wealth, and impact the lives of others in a positive way.

I'd like to share a few key stories from my journey—the times I chose to continue when most people would have quit. When things seem hopeless, there is a special power you can harness if you persevere. You must pass these tests over and over. It's a normal part of the process. There is always greatness, significance, fun, and contribution waiting on the other side.

The first story I want to share with you is about my first ten days in business. I followed a strategy called "10-a-day for 10 days." This meant that I would invite ten people each day to take a look at my online business for ten days in a row. I started on December 16, right in the middle of the Christmas season.

I would call each person and say, "I have something exciting I want to share with you. I met someone who is very down-to-earth and has had a lot of success with a global business project in over twenty countries. It's a billion-dollar brand, and I feel so blessed that he actually invited me into it. I started looking at people in my life, and I thought of you. I don't know if this would be for you, but I think very highly of you, so I want to share it. And even if it's not for you, I would love to get your opinion. Would you be willing to jump on another thirty-minute call tomorrow at 3 pm or 5 pm so I can explain all the details?"

This strategy worked so well. I was getting commitments the next day. I started to book my mentor's calendar. To open each call, I would say, "Is it okay if I get my mentor on the line because he is helping me through the process and has a great story?" I asked for permission, and my contacts said 'Yes.' It was so beautiful to connect my mentor and watch him give the presentation. Everything was outlined, clear, and done in thirty minutes. That's how I learned.

There is a term for this called "Making Millions on Mute." It's a great strategy because your friends trust you, but they do not respect you as a business leader. When you bring in an outside expert, you are combining trust with respect. With this dynamic, you can learn the presentation and be effective at the same time.

It took about two months to become independent and start doing presentations on my own. But I still spoke with my mentor every day to share what was going on with my prospects. That's one of the key points I want to share. Become independent on the presentation as quickly as possible, but stay close to the fire. Call your mentor daily and show them how hungry you are to build. This made me grow ten times faster. I spoke to my mentor almost every day for the first few years.

As I began building my team, I started to experience the 80/20 rule. This means that eighty percent of associates did not want to do the work, but they loved the products. And that is okay! Twenty percent of them took the business seriously like me.

There are five types of distributors. You need to know this in advance to save lots of heartache. Remember that you need all five to run a successful business. They are:

- Full-timers
- Part-timers
- Social distributors
- Wholesale buyers
- Seasonal distributors

Full-timers usually start out as part-time but they are very serious. They won't rest until they've made it big. They are rare, but they are out there. When you find one, teach them the system, and spend as much time with them as you can. It's important to get them independent with the presentation in the first two months but spend time mentoring them and connecting with them on all levels (personally & professionally). You literally cannot spend enough time with them. These are your main players. You only need three or four of them to become a six-figure earner yourself.

Part-timers are usually working towards the goal of full-time. Many love their job and will stay part-time for a while. These are your next wave of leaders. Mentor them and teach them the system so they can be independent from you as well. The part-timers who are ready to go to the next level will self-identify themselves over time.

Social Distributors love the meetings and conventions. They don't invite new people consistently, but they show up and enjoy the community. And that's okay. They will tell you that they want to make it big because they want your love, but they don't take action. Give them love and encourage them to attend events in your community. They will keep ordering the products. Don't judge them for their inactivity. Understand that they are social distributors who love the community, and they are an important part of a successful business.

Wholesale buyers start with the intention of building a business, but they decide that they don't want to put in the work or attend trainings. However, they love the products and continue to order. You can't stop them! Let them keep ordering and give them love too.

And finally, seasonal distributors work for a season and then leave. But they also come back as long as you don't make them feel bad when they leave. Keep the door open, and they'll return when they are ready.

One of the most important things to do in the beginning is invite people who have *more* influence than you. If they get started, they will grow faster than you. This happened to me twice in the beginning, and one of these success stories was my parents.

They enrolled and within twelve months had achieved a full-time income. My business was on fire thanks to them. If I had prejudged them and skipped them, I would not have had the same success.

During my first year, I made an effort to invite everyone I had ever met in my life. I spent hours going through yearbooks and old directories. I took list building very seriously. This is still important today. You must focus and invite every friend you have on social media. You will be surprised who says yes. Sometimes the people you pre-judge positively choose not to get involved. Sometimes the people you pre-judge negatively become your best team members. You never know. That's why you must invite everyone to take a look and let them decide for themselves. Every sparrow knows an eagle. You never know who they will introduce you to. That's why the networking game is so powerful.

After about a year, I had invited everyone I knew, and I needed to create more contacts. This was a struggle. We did not have social media back then, so I had to look for other ways.

Each day, after my working my job, I would go out and focus on meeting people. I was committed, but I was also horrible at it. In the beginning, I had business cards. I would walk up to people and say, "Hi, I'm Jared with XYZ company. We help people earn money on the side. Would you like more info?" I was like the plague. People ran from me. It did not work.

But I wasn't going to quit. I was going to keep adjusting until I figured it out. Everything is figure-out-able. Over time, you will make enough adjustments to get it right. The good news is that you only have to get it right once! Then, it's just a matter of repeating.

My next strategy was to be normal and strike up natural conversations. During that time, I would find common ground with people. I would complement them and follow with a question. I learned what to say, and I began to get phone numbers of interested prospects. I was getting better, but I wasn't a master yet.

One day I was at Walmart, and my goal was to talk to ten people. Apparently, that was too many because management started following me around. A feeling of horror washed over me as I watched the manager approach. He said, "Sir, we received a complaint from a customer that you were soliciting them in the store. You need to leave now." He escorted me out, and I felt like a criminal. I was kicked out of Walmart, and I wasn't welcomed back!

I remember driving home in my old car with no air-conditioning. It was over 100 °F outside, and I was melting. I felt dejected and defeated. I slammed my fist on the steering wheel and screamed at the top of my lungs in frustration.

Many would have quit and given up at that moment, but I doubled down. I had been successful before, and I would be successful again. I said to myself, "I don't care how long it takes. I will continue to adjust *until* I figure this out. I know I can do this. I believe in myself!" I eventually mastered the art of creating new contacts in public. Here's the exact strategy I still use to this day when I'm out:

Step 1: I ask what they do for a living and how long they have been doing it.

Step 2: I always ask what they like about their job and what they dislike about their job.

Step 3: I wait until the end of the interaction, and just before leaving, I say: "The reason I was asking about your job is because the company I work with is expanding. It's something that has _____ (mention their likes), but it doesn't have any of _____ (mention their dislikes). I'm sure you're totally happy with your job, and I don't know if you have all the qualities we are looking for, but if you'd like to exchange numbers, I'd be happy to get you some information."

When they say yes, I hand them my phone and say, "Type your number here and what's best time to call you tomorrow. I will text you before I call." I started getting phone numbers on demand. And I still get them to this day when I'm out in public.

I used the same philosophy to master social media. I took action and made adjustments *until* I mastered social media prospecting. That's when the real fun began. Using my social media strategy, I became the number one Associate Enroller in North America for my company. My wife and I received a huge trophy. It was a major highlight for our team and our career. But the most important part was all the lives that were changed in the process. For more information on how I build with social media, look me up on Instagram or Facebook. It's all there!

This is how we teach our teams today. The results have become exponential. What helped me breakthrough back then applies just as much now. Here is the formula.

Each day, take one step with prospecting activities and one step sharpening your knowledge with study. Abraham Lincoln once said, "Give me six hours to cut down a tree and I will spend the first four hours sharpening the axe."[4] Your personal growth strategy must be just as strong as your action strategy. You get sharp by taking action, and you get sharp by studying. You need to do both!

My personal growth strategy has been very simple: be on my team's weekly Zoom training webinars and attend live destination events in person. The weekly Zoom webinars are the glue to the latest and greatest strategies that are working right now. Over the years, I have made lifelong friends and connections through

---

4   "Abraham Lincoln Quotes," BrainyQuote (Xplore), accessed May 24, 2021, https://www.brainyquote.com/quotes/abraham_lincoln_109275.

these webinars. What's better is that I get to meet my team in person at the destination events every year. It's so much fun, and it makes for a rich life.

This brings me to the holy grail of personal development: The International Convention. This event happens every year for most companies and has made the biggest difference in my life. I became a master because I have never missed one in over fifteen years. Leaders attend live events and bring their teams with them!

My advice to you is simple: Follow the system. Be dedicated to webinar trainings and destination events with your company. Do income-producing activities every day and keep adjusting until you figure it out. If you control your attitude and activity over time, your success is guaranteed. Everything is figure-out-able and you can do this!

BIOGRAPHY

Jared Crebs is the #1 Community Builder in North America for his network marketing company. He specializes in helping new people create success with a cutting-edge mindset and social media strategies. He has been full-time in the network marketing industry for over a decade and loves the ability to change lives for the better. His passions include spending quality and quantity time with his wife and family, improving the professionalism of network marketing through improved processes and systems, and inspiring others to expand their imagination of what's possible for them.

Contact Jared Crebs via http://www.jaredcrebs.com/

CHAPTER 16

GRACEFUL TENACITY

By Josh Schonert

I believe my childhood prepared me for the challenges that I would go through later in life—challenges that shaped me into who I am today and where I've been able to work my way up, not only in the corporate world but also as an entrepreneur and business owner.

In the beginning, I was faced with my parents separating (I was not even two years old when it happened), which set off a chain reaction of emotional rollercoasters and uncertainty in my future. For years, my parents fought over who should be my primary guardian, and it weighed on me.

I didn't have many dreams and goals as a child and even into my teen years. I had some ideas, but they never really felt like things I could actually achieve. It's not that I was ever told I couldn't. I just didn't believe it at first.

After moving from California to North Dakota at the age of eighteen, I started my new adult life in a rough fashion. I got involved with the wrong crowd, which introduced me to a life of drugs and alcohol. This further led me to do some things that make me cringe anytime I think about it today.

The alcohol and the drugs started taking over my life, and I was barely sleeping most nights. I couldn't hold down a job, and I started getting into fights with my family and friends (I realize now they were trying to help).

Through all these issues, I always blamed others for my downfalls. It was my mother's fault that I didn't get to fulfill my dream of being a pro BMX racer, and her reaction to my teenage antics was so "extreme" that it caused me to move away. It was my father's fault for convincing me to move away from my home, which caused me to drop out of college, not hold down a job, and even get addicted to drugs. It was the police department's fault for pulling me over multiple times, which led me to lose my driver's license and spend thousands of dollars on legal fees and fines—even spending a night in jail. It was all my bosses' fault for all the jobs I couldn't hold down, causing me to jump from job to job.

The common denominator in all this was me. But I was too blind to notice it at the time, and I just kept making the same mistakes over and over for years.

During this time is when I had met Katie (my now wife). We dated on and off for a few years, mostly because I didn't realize what I had right in front of me.

As the years went on, no matter what I was putting us through, Katie was always with me through all of it. We moved away from the small town where I had been at the time and made our way to a bigger city in the state. This helped get me away from some of the drugs and alcohol, but it presented other challenges too.

I still had a hard time keeping a job, and all my entrepreneurial endeavors seemed to fall short, mostly because I didn't know how to deal with adversity yet.

Then, Katie and I had our first child. His birth brought on new goals and new challenges. There always seemed to be "more month" at the end of our money, and we were already on assistance to help pay for the necessities of having a child.

We struggled to keep up on our bills and were always behind or falling short, making up some bills one month, then others the next. No matter how hard we tried, we couldn't get ahead of our bills.

It was during this time that we faced our biggest challenges together.

Most people would think that we were living in some sort of Lifetime movie with everything we'd gone through and how we always seemed to come out fine in the end. One of them was when I was making my way home and had to stop at the grocery store to get the things we needed. It was about 9:30 p.m. on a summer evening, so it was quite dark outside. I stepped out of my car and immediately felt something up against my back as I was about to shut my door. "Money. Now!" The only thing that came out of my mouth was, "Really? Are you serious?" This man insisted that he'd shoot me if I didn't give up my money. I tried to reason with him, stating that the money I had on me was literally all I had for groceries and to feed my son, but he didn't care. He pushed harder and said that I had ten seconds. I told him my wallet was in my back pocket. He grabbed it, took my cash, and was gone as fast as he showed up.

I immediately called Katie, explained what happened, and told her to call her mother to ask for help. I didn't want to, but we just lost the only money we had for at least a week. At this moment, I felt something I never wanted to feel ever again: I felt like I was a failure and that I was letting my family down. Even though I didn't cause the situation, I felt like it was the poor decisions I'd made over the years that were catching up with me. And when I thought that was the worst it could get, we were blindsided again.

Katie had to have emergency surgery. She had what's called a "Staghorn" stone in her kidney that was causing her kidney to not drain properly and dangerously stretch out. The surgery went well, and they got out what they could. But what blindsided us was the bill. Due to the policies our insurance at the time had, they linked one of her previous appointments (before we had this specific insurance) with this procedure and claimed it was a "pre-existing condition." Because of this, they denied the claim for a surgery that was almost $100,000. This denial of the claim caused the hospital to send us a letter stating that we had thirty days to come up with ten percent of the bill: almost $10,000. We didn't have that kind of money. We pleaded with the insurance company and begged for their help, but they would not budge. We tried working out payment plans with the hospital, but they, too, were firm on their stance. We started receiving letters from lawyers that we had to pay or they were going to sue.

We had no choice. We hired a bankruptcy lawyer and filed. We lost everything. But, even through it all, we realized that this was a blessing. It gave us a clean slate to work on our finances and get in a better place. We both were working full-time jobs at this point, and things were looking up.

With the money we were making at the time, we moved to a nicer area and started working on putting together plans for our future. And while we had gotten to a better spot in our lives, we weren't prepared for what happened next: Katie was pregnant with our second child, and all seemed to be going well. Then she noticed some spotting. The spotting turned to bleeding, and then it was constant bleeding every day. We were told she miscarried and that she needed to wait it out. But we knew something was wrong. That was until the night came where she was going to make another ER visit and ended up needing to be taken there by ambulance. She was losing so much blood that she passed out in the bathroom and almost hit her head on the seat in the shower. I can honestly say that I've never moved as fast as I did that night.

I was lying in bed when it happened, and I don't even remember how I made it to the bathroom. All I know is that I made it there in time to catch her and prevent her from hitting her head in the shower, which very likely would have caused permanent damage. After emergency surgery to deal with the miscarriage, Katie came out okay, and we went on to have our second child a couple of years later.

Through all of these challenges, we had every reason to give up. We could have stopped and said, "That's it, I can't do this anymore." I've even seen people take drastic measures with their lives for lesser challenges. But as I said early on, I believe that the challenges I faced in my early years prepared me for what I was going to deal with later on in life.

I learned how to continue pushing forward, even when it seemed like the entire universe was pushing back. I became a believer that things would get better, even when it all seemed to be crashing down. Because of this, I never gave up, trying to do more and become a better version of myself. I was always looking to improve our situation—even working four jobs at one point.

Sure, I had to put many things on hold with my life, but that's what was necessary to get through it all. I learned that there are no special superpowers people are born with. In fact, it's something that we all have in us.

I had every reason to give up and stop pushing myself to do more. I could have given up and accepted that my life wouldn't amount to anything and that I would continue to struggle in that way, no matter how hard I tried to persevere. However, for years I've been inspired by a quote by a great author, Napoleon Hill: "Every adversity, every failure, and every heartache, carries with it the Seed of an equivalent or greater Benefit."[5] I recite that quote through every challenge to date.

---

5   "Napoleon Hill Quotes," BrainyQuote (Xplore), accessed August 9, 2021, https://www.brainyquote.com/quotes/napoleon_hill_121336.

I believe that no matter what we deal with, there's always something that's going to be better on the other side. That's how my marriage continues to be one of the best parts of my life. It's how I was able to work my way up to a six-figure position with a global software company, living my early childhood dream of being a computer engineer. It's how I was able to start seeing success with my entrepreneurial adventures and start building a legacy for myself and my family. And, it's how I ended up with the opportunity to write the words on this page that you are reading right now.

The thing is, all of these words are just that: words. It's what you do with these words that make the biggest difference.

For me, this is only a small part of a story that I believe can inspire people all over the world to do more with their lives. So many great things can happen in our lives, but we have to be willing to power through the challenges we may face to experience them. We have to give ourselves the ability to let our story play out while not stifling it at the same time.

We have to push ourselves to become more than we were yesterday and make it through any challenge that comes our way while also giving ourselves the grace that it won't happen overnight.

My friend phrased all this with two words, and I knew immediately that this was how I'd explain my experience and name this chapter: Graceful Tenacity.

BIOGRAPHY

Josh Schonert is what society would call a "Jack of all Trades." He has gone from working in lumberyards to being a health insurance consultant and even living out his dream of being a computer engineer. With all of these endeavors, the consistent theme has always been about helping others in any way he can. Through the years, he has earned a certification in Digital Marketing and Automation and completed several technical marketing courses, all in the name of helping others build their own brand online. Now he helps people all over the world and teaches them how they can utilize the internet to create the life they've always wanted. Josh enjoys golfing, fishing, biking, and spending time with his family. He currently resides in West Fargo, North Dakota, with his wife Katie and their two boys, Jeremiah and Owen.

Connect with Josh Schonert via https://jkschonert.com/links

CHAPTER 17

STEPPING UP TO THE PLATE

By Karen Dallman

Procrastination is a "virtue" I perfected over time. The ability to procrastinate till the last minute and still get whatever you need to get done in a reasonable amount of time can be daunting, yet in a weird sort of way, thrilling. You put pressure on yourself by putting off the inevitable till the last minute, and for some, that can be very stressful. For me, it is as if I am challenging myself to step up to the plate. Will I get it done? Will I strike out? Or will I hit that home run?

I remember sitting in the neurologist's office with my husband at the time. We visited many physicians over the course of eighteen months and still had no answers. Deep down, I knew the answer was not going to be good. I sent our children, Logan, who was ten, and Kendall, seven, to go sit out in the waiting room for a minute and then actually yelled at the doctor, "You know what it is! Just have the guts to tell us!" The answer was not what I expected. My husband, Ken, had amyotrophic lateral sclerosis (ALS). It was a terminal diagnosis that was going to make him progressively weaker and cause his muscles to waste away. Eventually, he was going to die. He was too young! How was this possible? From that moment on, our idyllic life was going to change. It was not something I felt I could go through, but I was going to have to step up to the plate. All I knew was that it was time to go into survival mode and make the most of our time left together as a family.

Ken was an amazing man. He was well-liked, easy-going, musically talented, a great father and husband, and a go-getter. He was the better half of me. I preferred to stand in the shadows, so to speak. Ken was a captain and paramedic with our local fire department. He was the first head commissioner on the Parks and Recreation Board for the city we lived in for nine years. He was able to write a grant while he was on that board, which was the start of one of many parks in our city. He volunteered to coach Little League and soccer even before our children were old enough to play. He belonged to service clubs and was part of a local band. He taught at our local community college as a certified instructor for the medic programs. He coordinated a dive rescue team that would search the river and lake in our area. Even during his final days, he campaigned to help get a bond passed to build a much-needed second junior high school. Saying he was vibrant and full of life doesn't seem like enough of a description.

I find it a bit ironic that I am a huge fan of baseball, and my husband ended up with ALS, commonly known as Lou Gehrig's disease (named after the famous baseball player who died from ALS). As a firm believer that everything happens for a reason, I was pretty sure that I was also introduced to a woman who also was diagnosed with ALS early in my medical career. We got to know each other better when she was placed in the nursing home across the street from the medical practice I worked at. She had no family and no one visiting her. I used to stop by every so often to visit. I remember praying I would never have to deal with someone personally with this disease because it is horrible to watch a person waste away. Little did I know, I was being prepared for my role in Ken's life.

The family routine changed as Ken's health issues progressed. Both my children stepped up to the plate as well. Kendall would help feed her dad or sit on his lap to drive the wheelchair when he was struggling with the controls. Logan would help his father in the bathroom or with showering. He also helped me load the wheelchair into the van until we were able to get a wheelchair-accessible van. Neither of them complained; they just did what they had to do. We did as much as possible together when we could.

It took three years for the disease to take over Ken, and when he died, I thought I was never going to survive. Life seemed a bit unfair, but I had two wonderful children. Logan was thirteen, and Kendall was ten. I had to seriously step it up. I was thirty-five, had no real career, and now, I was a mom *and* dad. At that point, my biggest goal in life was to not screw my kids up, and if I did anything I felt that might do so, I would hand them a dollar for their "therapy jar," just in case they felt they'd needed therapy later in life. I would say I was sorry, and we would move on. Both of my kids laugh about that today.

My need to be a good parent was something I felt deeply passionate about. Yet, I felt like a failure at times. It took a lot of courage to not just give up. However, failure was not in my vocabulary. My father taught me to never give up and always give my best effort. He would always tell me to 'go down swinging.' As you can see, the root of my love for the game started as a child. So, I did things I felt were necessary to help my kids. I learned to change the oil, brakes, and shocks in my car and perform basic mechanics through a cousin—skills which I passed on to both my kids. In turn, I looked forward to my 'Father's Day' card they gave me every year. I am proud of who they have become. Both my children graduated in the top 10 percent of their class. Both went on to college, have careers they are very good at, and are married with children. Life threw them a terrible curveball, and yet, they have turned out to be amazing individuals their father would be as proud of as I am.

I stayed with the physician's office where I was a medical assistant when Ken died. I did not go back to school for my RN as planned. However, I worked my way up to a supervisor position and eventually became manager for the practice. I ended up joining the Kiwanis Club Ken had belonged to and started doing my part in the community. I ran for the local school board and won! I was on my church council for many years and was also on the board of a non-profit community health clinic. I felt that becoming a volunteer as Ken had been would somehow make a difference in feeling as if I was a success. I have figured out that it is not how much you do that makes you successful, it is whether you give what you do your best effort.

I remarried eleven years after Ken died. To say that I am blessed is an understatement. My husband now is unlike any other. He is an internist with whom I have had the pleasure of working for thirty-five years. He is very compassionate, understanding, and not your typical physician. He likes to get his hands dirty, welds as a hobby, and sits on a foundation board that serves several communities in our state as well as two service organizations. He is unbelievably talented and very eloquent with his words. He saw me through some of my toughest times, became my best friend, and eventually, we decided to try marriage. Our beginning was a bit of a struggle, figuring out our positions on the playing field, but we eventually did, and I believe we complement each other.

Fast forward a few years . . . my son introduced me to network marketing. I can do anything for any length of time, and truthfully, to shut him up, I said yes, signed up, and did nothing for a year. My son, Logan, badgered me into going to my first training, and to say it was amazing is an understatement. To this day, that specific training was life-changing, and I have been hooked ever since. I am certain that training helped save my current marriage. It gave me a purpose I did not know I was searching for and made me realize this was something I dreamed of for years.

Over the nine years I have been a part of the network marketing concept, I have made some unbelievable friendships, learned from the best of the best trainers, and found mentors who may have not even realized they were making a more confident person. While I have not yet progressed with climbing the ranks of the network marketing company I am with, I have developed as a person. To me, that has been the most important part of my journey. I now have the confidence to move on, use this amazing concept to help others find themselves and their purpose, and have the courage to step up and become the leader I know I can be.

I have spent all my adult life looking for a purpose and feel like I was successful. Even though I went through the adversity of caring for and watching my first love die, raised two children who are amazingly successful and well rounded (goal reached . . . I did not screw them up), and was blessed with a second marriage to another amazing man, I continued to feel that was meant to do more, be more.

Bottom line: never give up on yourself. Continue to embrace your fears, and take whatever life throws at you. Get in that batter's box, wait for your pitch, make that decision whether you need to watch the first few go by, and learn from them. Or take a swing and possibly even the hit. Do not let the fear of the unknown take you down. All you can do is keep trying and keep swinging! Make it a grand slam!

BIOGRAPHY

Karen Dallman has made a career in the medical field as a CMA and practice manager for an internal medicine practice for over thirty-five years. Karen has two children whom she raised after the loss of her husband to ALS in 1997. She is a servant leader, volunteering in several service groups to help improve her community. Karen was introduced to network marketing in 2012 and found how important self-development is and encourages others to do the same. She uses her life experiences in both the medical field and as a previous widow to help others find the resources for their situations. Although Karen has been known to be "too busy and never slows down," she finds time for traveling, hiking, golfing, working to improve on other languages she is learning, and spending time with her grandchildren.

Connect with Karen Dallman via
https://linktr.ee/karendallman2021

CHAPTER 18

THE CURVE BALL

By Karla Munkel

We sat in the doctor's office for what seemed like an eternity. The door didn't move. The room was quiet, too quiet. I was beginning to believe it was taking too long for a quick second opinion. We kept waiting. My husband and I tried to make small talk, but it was meaningless conversation, and soon, the silence entered the room again. It was taking too long. I was becoming acutely and increasingly aware that I should be concerned, but I refused to let myself go there. Wait for the facts. Wait for the doctor. Everything will be fine. But really, why was this taking so long? Deep down, I knew something wasn't right.

We had just finished an echocardiogram on our baby who was twenty-three weeks gestation. We had been sent for a second opinion on the possibility of our baby having a hole in his heart. It was just a "possibility" and "quick second opinion." I didn't really think anything would come of it—just a routine check, and we would be on our way home.

The door finally opened. The doctor came in and asked if we knew why we were there. I was instantly annoyed by his patronizing question. Of course, we knew why we were there. I adamantly told him that it was just a precautionary measure to take a closer look at the baby's heart, as if the way I responded would make what was coming next obsolete. I knew this question was leading somewhere that wasn't good, but I wouldn't admit it. Wait for the facts.

As the doctor sat on his stool just a few feet away from us, he told us that our baby boy had multiple congenital heart defects. Our baby's heart did not form as it should have, and there was a possibility of further complications. The tears began to roll down my cheeks as I buried my head into my husband's shoulder. And just like that, life changed.

Life has a way of throwing curveballs at us. No one gets through this life without a few curveballs. How ready are you for the next one? Up until this moment in the doctor's office, we luckily hadn't had too many—just a few bumps in the road, but nothing like this. When we aren't ready for the curveball, it can take us out and knock us down physically, mentally, and emotionally. While leaving the doctor's office that day, I felt knocked down, defeated, and a bit lost. As I began to process the information later, I was reminded that we had a few things in our favor. First and foremost, we had our faith. I knew that would be essential for our road ahead. Secondly, I was reminded of an opportunity I had said yes to just two months earlier, a Plan B, if you will. I had no idea how significant that decision would become. The decision to become an entrepreneur, specifically in network marketing, two months earlier was a leap of faith, but one that I became instantly grateful for. Deep breath. It's going to be okay.

Truth be told, I never had the desire to be an entrepreneur. That was for other people to do, the risk-takers. I was certainly not a risk-taker. At this time, I was twelve years into my corporate career, with most of my career spent as an internal auditor.

While keenly aware of the risk, risk avoidance was more in my wheelhouse.

Fast forward five years (five trips to the Michigan children's heart hospital, two heart surgeries, and a thriving five-year-old boy), and I am now five years into my entrepreneurship journey. As much as I love having a plan B and diversified income from a financial side, if I had never made a single dime in entrepreneurship, I would still tell you the experience has been priceless. I don't know of any other path that requires so much of your true self, of stepping into your greatness. The intangibles in the last five years as an entrepreneur have developed character, confidence, grit, perseverance, optimism, mindset shifts, and a new perspective, just to name a few.

I hear a lot of success stories in the industry about lifestyle and monthly and annual incomes. One of the things not often shared is the intangible benefits of being an entrepreneur, specifically in network marketing. These are the benefits and values that if I had never made a dime in this industry, I would do it all over again. These are the priceless things, life lessons I can pass on to my kids, and when done right, these will not only impact their lives but the lives of their children as well. Teaching and sharing sound principles, values, mindset, and perspective to my kids . . . that will be my legacy. Money is temporary. With the right mindset and perseverance, you become limitless.

Before I dive into those non-tangible benefits, let me first be transparent that the path to success doesn't come without resistance. Let's talk about that. Resistance comes in all forms. It comes from within you, not wanting to do what you know you should. This is a *big* one. Don't underestimate this one. It can rear its ugliness when you least expect it, quietly sneak in, or be bold and overpowering. Consider this another curveball. The best way to prepare for this one and not let it take you down is through personal development. Invest in yourself through trainings, seminars, mentors, accountability buddies, and/or simply reading ten pages a day most days of the week. Don't be your worst enemy. Be your biggest cheerleader. In the beginning, you have to be your biggest cheerleader until you can fill the stands. So be the *best* cheerleader. You deserve it.

Remember I said resistance comes in all forms. Friends and family, that's another one. When you start down a new path, friends and family won't understand the changes you are making. They haven't heard what you've heard or seen what you've seen. I can't tell you how many times I've been asked the following: Why do you do "that?" You already have a full-time job while raising young kids. Don't you have enough on your plate? How do you have time to do that? Why don't you just enjoy what you have? You need to live in the present; don't focus on the future so much. Why are you always pushing for more?

If any one of these sounds familiar, you know exactly what I mean. The sting of the first time you hear this goes deep. You may question if people's perception is that you are in some way ungrateful for what you have, greedy, or unhappy. When the naysayers come out, the seeds of doubt get planted. At this point, you have a choice: water their opinions and allow them to grow or cut off the water supply and starve their opinions to the point of disappearance. Be on the lookout. These thoughts can knock you off your path for minutes, days, weeks, or even months. This is where perseverance, mindset, grit, and perspective come into play. Remember, you are creating your story—the story that is yours to create. Do you know that unsettled feeling in your stomach? That's your burning desire. Your burning desire was put there on purpose. It's up to you to put it into action. Don't let the naysayers stop you. Remember, greatness comes from doing the extraordinary, that which is beyond ordinary. In the beginning, the extraordinary can also seem unreasonable—even crazy. That's when you know you are on the right path!

So, let's get into it. What are those benefits that no one's talking about—those benefits that take you from mediocre to exceptional?

1. Mindset: Mindset is *huge*. Everything we do and don't do comes back to our mindset. Get it right, and you can have it all. Get it wrong, and you will remain stuck. Become an eternal optimist. I have found simply starting with "the good news is . . ." can completely change the approach and outcome. What you feed your mind matters. Who you surround yourself with matters. Just like our bodies need to be protected from junk food and chemicals, our minds need to be fed properly too. Simply reading ten pages a day most days of the week has been an absolute game-changer. It has broadened my perspective, allowed me to dream of the possibilities, and completely shifted my mindset.

2. Persistence: Success doesn't come from the first try. Success comes to those who don't quit, the ones that keep going, the ones that show up and do the work even on days they don't want to. Persistence takes you to amazing places and shows you how to break barriers. Keep going!

3. Grit: Want to develop a sense of grit? Become a network marketer! It's an easy target because many people haven't tried it, and those who have, likely failed. Ever notice it's usually not the successful people bringing you down? The failure rate is high in network marketing. If you're a numbers person and a risk-avoider, you may look at the stats and run. Stats are made of averages. Averages are the results of fifty percent above and below a number. Are you looking to be average or at the top? If you are looking to be average, be average. If you are looking to be at the top, spend more time rising to the top than worrying about failure rates. That's not you. Make failure irrelevant.

When you decide to no longer be average or take the good enough route, you are no longer concerned about averages. The risk of failure is no longer your concern.

4. Problem-solving: Problem-solving is one of the top-paid skills in networking marketing. This skill set separates the average from above average, the not-successful from the successful. The average person avoids problems; successful people see problems as opportunities. Become a master problem solver and watch your success grow. This skill has become an awesome parenting tool as well. Now, when my kids come to me with a problem, I don't solve it for them. I teach them to solve their own problems.

5. Confidence: Confidence in anything comes through repetition over time. Personal development and investing in yourself builds your confidence because it builds a sense of self. There's a true sense of peace that comes with being comfortable in your own skin—knowing and accepting that you have been perfectly created by your Creator with a divine purpose. I think of confidence in two forms: the internal confidence of self-being, worth, and purpose; and the external confidence of feeling equipped with the skill sets to tackle anything life throws at you, a sense of readiness to tackle the day!

When I teach my kids, or anyone for that matter, to leverage the power of the non-monetary values of entrepreneurship, they already have the power to become successful in all aspects of life, step into their greatness, and become unstoppable. They have created the ability to generate an income no matter what circumstances come their way. No matter what curveball tries to knock them down, they continue to thrive. I've seen this in action. I've seen team members take this equation to break through belief barriers to allow themselves to dream, to win. I've seen team members put these five principles together, bust through ranks, and even outrank me! That is what it's all about: helping others win. It's a gift like no other.

The curveballs will keep coming. This year, it was another heart surgery, braces for kids, dance classes, and about 100 other things. I'm ready for it all. I don't know what curve ball life will throw at you; I encourage you to be ready. Be ready to step into your greatness with all the possibilities this life has to offer. Every day is a gift with a purpose, your purpose. It's time for you to write your story. Build these muscles, and you will undoubtedly create success of your own—success that is yours to capitalize on in every way possible.

BIOGRAPHY

Karla Munkel is a wife and mom who believes a woman can have it all. She spent the first twelve years of her career in Corporate America before starting her journey in entrepreneurship while continuing to manage her corporate job and raise a family of four kids alongside her husband, Nate. Karla believes that through discipline, deliberate actions, and a firm mindset, entrepreneurship can be a gateway to not only creating the life you desire but becoming the person you have been created to become.

Connect with Karla Munkel via https://linktr.ee/karlamunkel

CHAPTER 19

THE DIAMOND IS IN THE ONION

By Kevin Baptista

It's nighttime; my friend and I are chilling at his house when we decide to go for a little joyride in his sister's car. We are on Brook Avenue, a one-way street, where I used to live with my mom, my brother, and my two sisters. This was in Roxbury, MA, the "hood" of Boston. That's where we used to play a game called "Which siren is it?" We could tell which kind of emergency vehicle was going by based on how it sounded. But back to me in the car, joyriding. My friend and I had only gotten a few seconds up the road when I noticed a car was right behind us. It seemed as though the driver was in a hurry, so I pulled over to plug in my iPod so that we could listen to some music. Believing everything was cool, I thought nothing of it. Then, the car pulled up right next to us, and the window started to roll down. My friend looked at me and asked if I knew who it was. I said I didn't. Then, before we could react, BANG, BANG, BANG! Eight or nine gunshots came our way. At that point, it was like a game of pinball. I immediately took off driving and hit the car in front of us. I turned right, and I hit a car parked on our right, then another car. I wasn't sure if the shooters were chasing us or not, so I put my foot down and drove off as fast as I could. I drove and drove, and all the while, my mom was trying to call me on my phone because she felt something was wrong. But I couldn't answer the phone. My friend was scared and thought he might have been shot.

We eventually got to the next safest place we knew; his grandmother's house. But when we got out of the car, we were suddenly surrounded by police cars. The officers asked us where our gun was. They could not believe we were not part of a gang and had simply been in the wrong place at the wrong time. They took us in for questioning. Having to ride in the back of the police car felt terrible, especially as I knew I didn't belong there. But the officers believed us and let us go home after about half an hour. I got home to a big hug from my mom. Tears started pouring down my face.

After that, my mission became to get out of the "hood" and provide a better way of living for my mom. Such external experiences that are out of our control happen to us throughout life. But it is, and will always be, our responsibility as individuals not to point the finger at anybody but ourselves when they have negative repercussions for us. I believe an angel was watching over us that night. Eight or nine gunshots were directed straight at us, and neither of us got hit by a bullet! There were big bullet holes in the passenger-side window. Thank God for tinted windows! None of the glass was shattered, either.

Our lives had been spared, a blessing for which I will always be truly grateful, and I don't think that was a mere coincidence. I was only a teenager when that happened, and I continued to hang out with the wrong people and put myself in situations I wanted no part in. I knew I had to smarten up.

Eventually, I was introduced to my girlfriend, and we've been together for ten years now. We have a six-year-old daughter together and a beautiful dog. She saw something in me back then, for sure. She never hesitated to tell me how she felt about the neighborhood I was living in and that she wanted me to get out. But being a teenaged boy filled with testosterone and trying to impress everybody, I didn't listen. I didn't want to be called whipped. Besides, my friends thought I didn't want to hang out with them anymore. I was trying to please everyone. I've since learned that you can go crazy trying to satisfy everyone. I'm not saying to be an asshole and not listen to what people have to say, but make sure your energy levels are intact. Creating a better you will always help you ride to the top.

Back then, though, I had a sense of entitlement, as though people owed me something or I owed them an explanation. I had feelings of guilt and shame. I ignored anyone who gave me more than just material things, especially a special someone who gave me their heart. I took advantage of that person, never really sincerely apologizing for my behavior. It amazes me that my girlfriend has stuck around for as long as she has. I know I will make more mistakes, but I don't want to repeat the ones I've already made. I've learned I'm not perfect, but I believe I can turn things around more quickly now. I think of those awkward nights when we end up not talking, or when I'm convinced she's in the wrong. That's my ego taking over again! Because of it, our relationship has suffered in the past, and once it got so bad, she actually broke up with me. At that point, there was so much shame and guilt inside me, I got really low, and things seemed dark. I knew I had to step up and be the man I knew I was capable of being. I was and always will be a role model for my daughter. I can't give up on our relationship and take the easy way out. I chose to man up and take responsibility for everything.

It was important to me to have a place of our own, where our daughter can grow up and we are all together as a family. She is with us at all times and soaks up everything she sees and hears. It's important to understand that kids soak up everything. They soak up how we act in certain situations and what we say. It is up to us as adults to lead by example. Our parents did the best they could with the knowledge they had. We can choose to blame our parents, or everyone we think has wronged us when something bad happens, but that will not allow us to free our spirits and take responsibility for ourselves for what has happened.

My girlfriend was someone with whom I could have a different kind of conversation than anyone else; we talked about things like finding a better life outside the "hood." She liked me to take the bus to her parent's house at night after I got off work at one in the morning. She constantly showed me how much she cared. While I might be at a place mentally where I feel I can take on the world, that doesn't happen without experience. Every situation is a chance for growth. It's as if you are beginning the process of peeling back the layers of an onion.

I wasn't in any gangs back then, but gang problems became my problems because I chose to hang out with them. My mom has always shown me love and support and has done the best she could for me. She will forever be an inspiration to me. My perspective really changed in 2017 when two brothers by the name of Guy and Ilan Ferdman of Satori Prime offered amazing courses on spirituality and a great Facebook group that I could open up and really be myself. That's where I learned that vulnerability is strength. Different inspirational videos by Gary Vee and Eric Thomas, and motivational books, like *Think and Grow Rich* by Napoleon Hill (1937), *A Happy Pocket Full of Money* by David Cameron Gikandi (2015), and *Rich Dad Poor Dad* by Robert Kyosaki (1997). The book *Reality Transurfing* by Vadim Zealand (2005) has been helpful on my journey. Although these books and the people behind them have greatly influenced my life, none of what's in them means anything unless you're prepared to take action. With action, you feel some pressure. Pressure you put on yourself!

Pressure is what starts the process of forming a diamond. It takes an insane amount of pressure to form a diamond. Of course, I don't mean taking action once and thinking you've done all you need to and that everything will be okay. Say you've hurt someone; you can't expect them to forgive you right away. There is a reason why people say actions speak louder than words. There is always one thing we can do to better our life experience and the experience of people around us. A hell of a lot of self-reflection and taking ownership of our actions is what takes you to the next level of self-development.

Yes, men do cry. If you don't cry, then you aren't human. Yes, I blame myself for messing up all those times in my relationship with my girlfriend, but I choose not to dwell on that. If I'm sad, I talk about it. If you don't have a friend or a partner to talk to, there are plenty of Facebook groups out there where you can connect with others. It's not crazy to talk to yourself, either; by doing that, you're creating a relationship with yourself. Every day, you should be thinking about what you can be grateful for. For instance, maybe you woke up today and had to go to the grocery store to get your food? Well, be thankful you're not out on the farm trying to protect your crops and wait for them to grow before you can eat. Social media is fantastic, and we can connect with each other much more rapidly nowadays. But don't get into the habit of going online and comparing yourself or your lifestyle with others. I used to do that; I'd get jealous every time I scrolled through Facebook or Instagram. All that matters in life is our level of happiness. If we're not satisfied with our circumstances, it is up to us to change them. Don't just wait around and hope things will change. Make a conscious decision to be a little better every day. If you slip up or, say, don't go for that walk you said you would, don't beat yourself up. Try again.

Everyone's path is different. I had to realize that for myself. My girlfriend took me back, but our relationship is a continuous process. You can be sure there are people out there who believe in your abilities. Positive change starts with you. What matters is now, this very moment. We can always learn from the past. And guess what? The way we approach one thing tends to be the way we approach everything. The level of effort we put into our relationships directly reflects how our finances shape up, or the way we feel about our health and weight. We *can* get better every day. To grow as people, we have to be prepared to step outside our comfort zone. I know we've all heard that many times, and it turns out to be true. Really evaluate the things you are willing to do and be open to others who are trying to help you along the way. Be creative in your approach. I like to think of life as a video game, but we don't get endless respawns.

Our self-awareness needs to continue to grow. I need to continue to give myself credit for the growth that has taken place in me, and you should do the same. It's not about the amount of dollars in your bank account, but the level of happiness you feel. Are you adding value to the people around you? I remember those days of looking up to the stars and wanting a better life for my family and myself. It's great to have a vision and goals you want to accomplish. But what is the lifestyle you want that will lead to you accomplishing those goals? Do you want to stay talking with those same five people about how good that girl looks? Instead, you should go get her number. Do you constantly blame others for your shortcomings, so, say, if she hasn't washed the dishes, I'm not going to do it either? I'm done waiting. I'm done making excuses. I can look at the past with a smile because it has brought me here. How can I expect to succeed if my foundation isn't strong? Let's create a better definition of success. I'm not going to wait until a goal is fulfilled to choose to be happy. I choose it now! If you do the same, you will feel light! Negativity is always around us, and we can't control how others view the world, nor should we try to. We have the light within us. It's like peeling back the layers of that onion and looking inside; that's where we will find that diamond.

Pressure is good. Our relationships directly reflect how we feel about ourselves. With that light, we can brighten a dark room. I love to give thanks in the morning and at night for everything in my life, to take it all in deeply. Now, I listen to complaints. Were dishes not done? That's on me. Laundry needs doing; that's on me too. When you gain a hold on a feeling, you will know what to do. Never feel too high or remain too low. Life is perfect in that regard, so just go ahead and feel it all, every emotion. And most importantly, have fun with your life experience. Why not let it be you that delivers that smile to someone? Are you willing to change your life? Yes!

BIOGRAPHY

Kevin Baptista is the co-author of an anthology with Matt Morris. He grew up in Boston, MA, where he experienced hardships and gang violence. Throughout that experience, he learned to strive for something greater; a life of inspiring others to be their best selves. His passions are spending quality time with his family and improving as a human being on a daily basis. His mission is to empower people and show them it's never too late to go after their dreams.

Connect with Kevin Baptista via
https://linktr.ee/buildinganempire

CHAPTER 20

BREAK THE MOLD

By Kimberly O'Neill

The most important "job" I find myself fortunate enough to have is that of being a parent. I'm a mom, and the majority of my decisions now reflect that role and my desire to do it well. I'm also an overachiever. I was always an overachiever. When it came to sports, I excelled. When it came to the military, I excelled. When it came to graduate school, I excelled. Pretty much every goal I set for myself, I achieved and excelled. But I rarely took time to celebrate the wins and consistently looked for the next goal. Something was always missing.

I still had a voice in the back of my mind saying, "You have to do more! You aren't doing enough! And what you are doing isn't good enough! Be better! Do more! You aren't there yet! It's not enough!" I also had a strong desire to be liked and accepted, and this voice would tell me things like, "You just don't fit in. You aren't like everyone else. You have to change for people to like you because you aren't thin enough, fit enough, smart enough, interesting enough, fun enough, and likable enough. You just aren't enough. Do more. Be more." I don't know where this voice came from or why it plagued me virtually my entire life, but I know I'm not alone.

I also can pinpoint the events that led me to really challenge this voice and reach a point where I am my own voice, where I write my own script, where I don't need the approval of others, and where I really do love myself for who I am, where I've been, and who I am becoming. It definitely didn't happen overnight. In fact, I have been a work in progress for more than a decade, with the real fruits of my labor finally coming into bloom since around 2020.

In 2004, I found out I was pregnant. I was in the middle of school for my new career as an officer in the Air Force, which wasn't ideal because the training was demanding. A few weeks in, I underwent emergency surgery to save my life when the pregnancy caused my fallopian tube to rupture. I lost the baby and half of my fertility in the blink of an eye.

While nobody said I couldn't feel grief for the trauma or that I couldn't mourn the loss of my child, I worried that allowing myself to feel it would lead to a breakdown and that a breakdown—given the requirements of my field—could potentially end my career. So, I focused on my training so intently that I graduated #1 in my class. Fast forward to my first duty assignment, I was blessed with a second chance at pregnancy, only to be devastated again. This time, I focused on work and was on rotation for deployment in a matter of weeks.

These events were undoubtedly the catalyst for what came next. It wasn't until I was out of the military, remarried, and trying to conceive again that I recognized the damage, danger, and lingering pain that was never addressed.

Broken. Unworthy. Failure. Not enough. These are just a few of the pervasive thoughts that preceded what I would call an absolute breakdown and tearing apart of who I thought I was, followed by choices, risky behaviors, and self-sabotage to a level that can only be described as perhaps an attempt to live up to the useless and broken unworthiness I felt inside of myself.

I had decided that doing all the right things and being excellent didn't matter. So, I did things that were in stark contrast to who I was at the core—things that would allow me to justify the shame and disappointment I felt in myself in a way that put me in control. I denied my integrity as if it were a way to punish myself for being inadequate. This was hands down the most difficult, uncomfortable, and borderline hopeless time I can remember ever experiencing in my life.

Fast forward to the present day, and I will tell you that I have given birth to two incredible, beautiful miracle children who are my life, heart, and soul. My daughter, in no uncertain terms, saved my life. I was in a downward spiral of drinking and partying, and I was in a very toxic relationship that perpetuated the self-destructive cycle. I was running.

I had convinced myself that my choices up to that point got me exactly what I deserved and that I was unworthy of any real kind of healthy love. She was unplanned and unexpected and truly the gift that drove me to get my life together again.

Focusing on her, my own fog started to clear, and I started remembering who I was and who I wanted to be. I started making decisions that brought me more in line with my integrity. I landed a government job, bought us a house, and ended my toxic relationship with her father. I wasn't completely there yet, but I was getting there.

Eventually, I remarried. Fertility issues struck again, but this time, when the self-talk threatened to take a turn for the worst, I sought help to avoid the catastrophic shutdown that I experienced before. Recognizing and honoring that need was the first step to a long road of healing and growth.

After seven years, three losses, two more emergent surgeries, and multiple failed attempts with in-vitro fertilization, I decided continuing to try was no longer healthy for me. As irrational as I knew it was, feelings of inadequacy and the perception that I was broken or damaged made me feel less of a woman and undeserving of happiness. I was losing myself, and enough was enough.

Overachievers like to be in control, but this was something I could not control. So, I would distract myself with work or take more classes—things that would help me feel accomplished. After a few years, my love for my work had lost its luster when the environment became very toxic. I found myself avoiding interaction as much as possible. I would show up, shut my door, and keep to myself. At the end of the day, I would wind down with a glass of wine, or sometimes, a bottle. I felt lonely and lost.

What was the point? I felt no sense of purpose anymore. I felt like I was just going through the motions of life and certainly was not as present as I could have been at home as a result. Something was missing. Again.

I wanted to spend more time with my family. I wanted to have more freedom in my days. I hated punching a clock. I felt like my life was wasting away and passing me by while I sat in that office. But it was a "good" job, with stability, benefits, and opportunities for growth, right? I should feel grateful, not resistant, right? What was wrong with me?

Then in 2016, I attended a training where I learned the term "cognitive dissonance," which refers to the state of discomfort felt when two or more modes of thought contradict each other. This created a major epiphany for me, and this is where my life took a major warp speed turn for the better.

I had a good job, but it could never give me the life I knew I wanted. It provided stability but not freedom. It provided an opportunity but not the kind I wanted. I had ideas I wanted to pursue, but they conflicted with my career. I sat in that training, and the idea hit me like a tidal wave: "I have to quit my job. I'm going to quit my job!"

Now, I don't recommend making rash life decisions! But to be honest, I had written my resignation letter two years prior. I just hadn't followed through with it! I finally had the courage to execute the action! I was going to quit my job and pursue my entrepreneurial endeavors. I let go of that toxic relationship, too, and I felt a million times lighter.

Less than a month later, I was pregnant with my son: no intervention, no treatments, no medication, and no issues. At forty-one years old, I had a miracle baby boy who has been my heart and soul ever since. The gift of my children, combined with my realization that I get to create my own destiny, led to even more personal development, which in turn led to more opportunities.

I had an unquenchable thirst for knowledge. I read dozens of books on self-awareness, parenting, childhood development, conscious parenting, the subconscious mind, body language, intuition, energy, and being present. I went to school for life coaching and neuro linguistic programming. I attended personal development seminars, and I was eventually offered a position as a contract leadership development trainer, where I got to choose my own schedule and was well-compensated for my time and knowledge.

Then, in 2020, I said goodbye to my final toxic relationship, alcohol. It started with a thirty-day alcohol experiment to evaluate and challenge my thought processes and behaviors around alcohol. About two weeks into the experiment, my mindset changed so much that I literally had no desire to ever consume alcohol again. I not only didn't want it, but I became repelled by the thought of it. The last thing I ever want my kids to feel is that mommy needs wine to deal with being their mom.

I started to save the money I would've been spending on wine. I thought I'd do something nice for myself at the end of the thirty days, but 500+ days later, I had saved $3,696. It was time to do something epic to celebrate. So, I gathered up my kids, and we hit the road for a cross-country adventure! We spent two full weeks traveling, camping, exploring, laughing, and experiencing our world in ways we'd not done before. Our time was flexible, as were our destinations. Our only objectives were freedom and adventure.

Success looks different to different people. But for me, I'm literally living the dream. I've always been someone who would see challenges and be of the FITFO mindset. FITFO to me meant "Figure It the F*&S Out!" Stop complaining, stop whining, stop focusing on the obstacles, and just figure out how to get it done. But now, more often than not, it means "Focus Inward To Find Opportunity."

Focus inward, because nobody knows what is best for us more than ourselves. If we listen for it, look for it, and feel for it, we know what decisions are right for us. They may not make sense to other people, and that's okay. It involves letting go of any expectations we think other people have of us, breaking out of the mold of living life in a prescribed fashion, and confidently following our own path.

It's asking yourself questions like, "How is this serving me? What might serve me better? What kind of internal dialogue am I having about this? Do I like the way this script is going, or should I change it? What would I rather hear? Does this feel authentic? Am I experiencing cognitive dissonance? If so, why? What's off? What would be more in line with me? What is the reality of this situation if I remove all judgment?"

This approach has enabled me to eliminate toxicity from my life. It helped me break the mold of who I thought I should be, allowing me to embrace who I am and who I want to be.

Focus inward, because being self-aware and authentic is key to everything. We cannot lead anyone until we can lead ourselves, and living our own lives authentically is one of the best examples we can set for anyone. Figuring out what that means is worth the effort.

BIOGRAPHY

Kimberly O'Neill is your basic badass. She has magnetic enthusiasm and dynamic life experience with over twenty years in leadership development and lifestyle transitions. She has championed hundreds of workshops and coached thousands of people to face their fears, obliterate excuses, and level up to reach their goals. Kimberly served in the Air Force and government before transitioning to the network marketing industry, where she leads large teams and coaches individuals to succeed. Commitment to family and service to others led her to entrepreneurship as a speaker, author, and coach. She has inspired audiences from one to more than 2,000 and is known for her ability to motivate and drive people into action. Passionate about personal growth and mental toughness, Kimberly is highly credentialed and consistently pushes herself to new levels. She works from home in upstate NY, where she homeschools her children, maximizing all that life has to offer!

Connect with Kimberly O'Neill via
https://linktr.ee/kimberlyoneill

CHAPTER 21

P.M.A.

By Kristen Monegato

I was an eight-year-old girl when my parents moved our family into our new home. The first piece of furniture that would go into the house was a 9' pool table. At that time in my life, I had no idea how impactful this pool table would be twenty years later. How could I? I was only eight years old! I recall memories of my brother and me running around it, playing silly games, and hitting the pool balls around the table, having no clue what we were doing or how to play the game. In my later years, my dad would teach me a few things as well as give me a few tips.

Fast forward thirteen years, I was going to college and studying pre-med. A friend and I were desperate for a break, so we decided to take every Friday off from our studies, go to a pool hall, and have a few margaritas to let loose. It became our weekly ritual and a great way to escape all the pressures of college. We had a fantastic time shooting pool and meeting some amazing people with whom I'm still friends to this day. After a few months, we were approached by a league operator who asked us if we would be interested in joining a league. I quickly agreed as I was falling in love with my new hobby.

Growing up as an athlete, I was super competitive, and this league sparked a fire in my belly that I hadn't had since high school. After a few weeks of playing, I quickly realized there was a huge sub-culture, and I wasn't good at all. I was getting beat left and right, and I hated that. There were a lot of really good amateur players out there and I was determined to become one of them. So, I began my journey to become a better player, and I was going to search high and low for that "magic bullet."

After playing in that league for six years and winning a regional women's tournament, I wanted to elevate my game even further. I joined a different league and met even more skilled players. I thought shooting with them was going to help raise my game even more. I found out there were different ranks (or statuses) you can achieve. And in order to achieve a particular rank, you had to compete at the state or national level. I knew immediately I wanted to go to nationals, and I set a goal to become a "National Master," which meant placing in the top 4 percent of the women's open division.

I was so excited. I knew what I wanted to accomplish, and I wanted to share my excitement and goals with the people to whom I was close. Instead of being received with love, support, and encouragement, I received looks and feedback from people with disgust. Like, what was I thinking? Someone even said, "Why are you wasting your time on something that's so worthless in your life?" "Why don't you put your energy into something that will benefit you?" "You're never going to do anything with pool." I had more people throwing daggers at my dreams than you can imagine. Have you ever had anyone in your life destroy your dreams in the blink of an eye?

I did not care what anyone had to say. I loved playing pool, and I wanted to accomplish my goal of becoming a national master. NOTHING WOULD STAND IN MY WAY! NOTHING!! Starting in October of 2008, I sacrificed the following eight months, consistently shooting six days a week, eight hours each day, working on my game. I got a coach, bought several books and DVDs for learning drills, banks, and kicks, shot execution, and learned how to control the cue ball. You name it, I wanted to learn it. I kept a journal to document my progress and see the improvements I was making. I never would've guessed how much time and dedication was required to be successful at this game. If I learned five things, there were two million more things to go. It dawned upon me that I really didn't know anything at all. I was reaching for everything I could get my hands on to be the player I wanted to be.

In May of 2009, I made it to my first national tournament. I was a nervous wreck. I walked up to the table for my first match, put my cue together, shook my opponents' hand, and wished her good luck. It was a race to five, which meant the first person to win five games would move on to the winners' bracket. The loser would have a very long road ahead of them. I had put in all this time studying the game, and I was looking my opponent in the eye, worried about losing. We were trading games, and after some time, it was 4–4. Whoever won this last game moved to the winners' side. I felt immense pressure to win so I wouldn't have twice as many matches to play to get to the finals. I was hot and shaking, my heart was racing, and I was on the verge of downward spiraling with negative thoughts on how I wasn't shooting the way I knew I could or should. That was a BIG wake-up call as I realized that no amount of "magic bullets" could win the match for me. I needed to dig deep within my soul and have the grit to pull off this first win.

Reflecting back on this match, this was a pivotal moment for me. I didn't realize it at the time, but I was either going to win and come out of that match with tremendous confidence or lose and feel totally defeated. My opponent and I had the same goal in mind; it was just a matter of who was going to capitalize on the opportunity that was given to them first. And with all the heart I could muster up, I had my opportunity and won! The journey was nowhere near over. It had only just begun. I had gained some confidence to go into my next matches knowing I had every ability to dig deep when I had to and when fear of losing was not an option. As I went through the tournament, I faced women of all different playing abilities. I had to fight through, match after match after match, and with the same fire, passion, heart, grit, and focus as I did in the last game of my first match.

I was winning. What an amazing feeling! The further I got in the tournament, though, the tougher the players, and the easier it would become to find any excuse to lose. You play for twelve to fourteen hours each day, one match after the next, with little breaks until you're near the end. That first day, I had to push myself through anxiety, exhaustion, hunger, negative thoughts more than I could've ever imagined. I had to have the heart and desire to accomplish what I came out there for. I focused in on my goal and eliminated all the distractions and excuses from my mind. You must believe in yourself. Otherwise, you won't have the confidence to go out there and get out of your own way. And how you're feeling on the inside is a direct reflection of how you're going to play. So, I decided I wasn't going to give up and before I knew it, I had made it to the final board, and I was in the top sixteen out of 420 women. I had become a National Master!

I realized everything I did was absolutely necessary to get me here. I needed to improve my skill set to know what I needed to do on the table. I had to get a coach, I had to do drill after drill after drill, I had to track my progress by logging in my results, I had to read, I had to sacrifice my time. But even all that wasn't enough. The intangible was my heart, my desire, my drive to win when everything and everyone is against me... When you're backed against the wall and you're down 2–4 in a race to 5, are you going to fight with everything you have to win? Or are you going to let the negativity and all the excuses creep in and lose?

In life, just like in pool, you can create a lot of excuses as to why you can't achieve your goal. I could've easily given up— even from the very beginning when people were telling me what a dumb, worthless, waste of time this pool hobby was going to be. I could've given up when I felt tired, mentally broken, nervous or anxious, down in my match and fighting to get back up. Excuses are easy—they're all around us. The table is too slow, the lights aren't bright enough, the balls are dirty, I'm hungry. I hate my boss, I'm too busy, I work another job, I have 3 kids, I'm sick. Being successful either on the pool table, or in business, takes a calm confidence and your mind, body, and soul being in total alignment. If any one of those is off, it doesn't work. Your muscle memory flops, a negative thought pops in your head…you will fail. It's the same thing in business. You have to remain calm and confident and believe in yourself that what you set your mind to, you can accomplish.

Everyone is busy and everyone has something that they're going through. What makes you different and great is that you do what no one else wants to do and that's hustle, fight and grind through when excuses are easily come by. Ironically, playing pool and setting that goal for myself gave me the greatest life lesson I could ever walk away with. NEVER GIVE UP ON YOURSELF! Only you can create the life you want to live.

I can now look back on all those people that doubted me and smile knowing I did something I can be really proud of. How would I feel if I had listened to them? They would've won… not me! And I would have never known what I could achieve or that I could become a nationally ranked master . . . how utterly disappointing! So, if there are people in your life that doubt you or make you feel ashamed for the life you're trying to create, leave 'em behind. You do you because no one else is going to. And if you're choosing NOT to do something because someone is putting doubt in your mind, I implore you to go after what you want. Otherwise, you may never know what you're capable of becoming. Put your mind to something. It does not matter how big or small it is. Your mind is the strongest tool you can tap into to get whatever you want. You have to simply believe in yourself enough to get it.

Achieving that goal in pool gave me the confidence to know what I needed to do to be successful in life and in business. And what it takes is positive mental attitude (P.M.A.), heart, fight, desire, tenacity, and perseverance. All of those things that champions have—successful people have. It takes all the same qualities to reach the top. Are champions always successful? Do they have their ups and downs? Of course, they do! But one thing they NEVER HAVE is QUIT.

Little did I know that the pool table in my parents' house was going to teach me all these life lessons—lessons that I can carry with me in business and pass along to my daughter. So, I ask you: What's your pool table?

BIOGRAPHY

Kristen Monegato is a God-fearing, loving wife and mother, who has developed a multiple six-figure income as an entrepreneur in sales and business development over the last ten years. She is a fierce athlete and competitor and uses her knowledge and experience from that to help others create solutions to problems and help people learn how to become the leaders they want to be. Kristen obtained a full-ride scholarship for music on the bassoon and graduated from the University of Illinois at Chicago with degrees in psychology and biology. She is a co-author in the Journal of BioSystems for her research in retinal physiology and also studied cognitive behavior at UIC Medical Center for individuals suffering from schizophrenia. Kristen loves to travel, take adventures, play competitive pool, workout, scuba dive, snowboard, read, enjoy wine, and spend quality time with her husband, daughter, and the people she loves.

Connect with Kristen Monegato via
https://linktr.ee/moneycatboss

CHAPTER 22

FIND YOUR "WHY"

By Matt Sharpe

I was raised in a rural area of North Carolina, fifteen minutes from anywhere. Fresh air, wildlife, and quiet were normal to me. I had two wonderful parents who worked hard and provided everything I needed. They taught me that family is the most important thing in life and to be kind to everyone. I couldn't have asked for a better childhood. I had an abundance of friends with whom I enjoyed hanging out. A lot of people would say that my life was perfect.

I didn't think it was. Don't get me wrong. I loved my family, my home, and my friends. However, there was something that always made me feel inferior. I was constantly bullied for my ears since I started school. My ears stuck straight out instead of being tucked to the side of my head like most people. I was called Dumbo, like the little elephant in the Disney movie. I was asked if I could hear things miles away. Think of anything that could be said about someone's ears, and I guarantee I've heard it before.

After years of being picked on for my ears, I decided to have a surgery called otoplasty to correct them during winter break in eighth grade. The pain after surgery was excruciating—but not as painful as the years of bullying. When we all returned to school, I was shocked to find out that none of the people who bullied me all those years even noticed my ears were different. They asked if I had gotten a haircut! Really? A haircut?

At that moment, I realized that it wasn't my ears that caused the bullying. It was my lack of self-confidence. My reaction to their hurtful words fueled them to continue picking on me. From that point on, I decided never to let someone's words degrade my self-confidence.

I always had good grades in school, but the fire to be the best was burning hotter than ever. I went to high school and graduated valedictorian of my class. I received a full academic scholarship to college and entered my first semester within a few credit hours of being a sophomore. I was on top of the world. At least it appeared that way.

I struggled through my first couple of years in college. Not because the classes were too hard but because I didn't have a sense of purpose. I had already achieved my mission: to prove to all those bullies from my childhood that I could do anything.

Fortunately, I met a young woman who helped me get back on track. She was my confidant, my rock, and my biggest supporter. She's the reason I finished college. I couldn't bear the thought of disappointing her, so I put my head down and finished my degree in 2002. We married the year before I graduated, and this year, we celebrated our twentieth wedding anniversary. I'm thankful every day that God put her in my path. We have two beautiful daughters, and our life is wonderful. But it hasn't always been wonderful.

Fast forward from college graduation to 2008. My wife had taken a leave of absence from teaching for one year to be home with our then-toddler and newborn daughters. The economy was in the tank, and I was working as a construction equipment sales rep. I wasn't making many sales, but the bills kept coming. We were broke and didn't know what to do. I remember sitting in my parents' driveway preparing to come home when my dad handed me a check so we could pay our mortgage.

I remember thinking, "How can I be in this situation? I've achieved all these great things in my life, but I can't even pay my bills. and I might lose my house!" I broke down in tears because I was supposed to be the provider. I was the one responsible for my wife and daughters' well-being, and I had failed. All the work, all the late hours, all the effort . . . and I'm relying on my parents to keep a roof over our head.

The promise I made to myself all those years ago that I would never let someone's words or actions lower my self-confidence had disappeared. I still didn't let others affect my opinion of myself, but I never realized that my biggest "bully" was me! I was the one convincing myself that I wasn't good enough and that I was a failure. I had become my worst enemy. It affected my work, my family life, and my desire to succeed. Feeling like a failure is a powerful thing. It can destroy you, or it can make you evaluate your life and make changes.

Thank goodness I chose the latter and decided to truly look at myself. I realized that I was not a failure just because things were not going according to plan. I was not a failure because times were tough, and we didn't have much money. I still had a loving family, an incredible wife, and two precious daughters. I overly focused on material things instead of the things you can't put a monetary value on. The most precious gifts anyone could have . . . I had!

Now what I needed to do was figure out what I could do differently to create more financial stability and less stress for myself and my family. Why were things not working out? What am I doing wrong? It hit me like a ton of bricks. It wasn't that I didn't work hard; it was that I didn't have a "why" that motivated me to cast off my doubts and push forward.

Your "why" is essentially your reason for doing the things you do. It's the "Why am I doing this?" Your "why" can help you set defined goals and reach them because you have a clearly defined reason for succeeding.

I analyzed what had motivated me in the past to push myself and have the never-quit attitude I had in high school. The light bulb went off, and I realized that for years, my motivation was proving to everyone else that I could make it. It was all about me and what I could accomplish. Don't get me wrong, I cared deeply for my family and friends, but everything I did to be successful was about me, not them. It was a hard pill to swallow. For years I thought I was doing the right things for my family, and I was, but it wasn't for them; it was for me and my constant desire to feel worthy. That little boy who had self-doubt and low self-esteem still lived rent-free in my head.

I needed a better "why." I found it one evening while eating dinner with my wife and daughters. As we all sat around talking about our day, it dawned on me. The people sitting at the kitchen table are my "why." It's no longer about what I can accomplish for *myself*, it's what I can accomplish for *us*. The most liberating thing I have found in my life is realizing that my success is for something bigger than me. My "why" is providing my family with the best life possible and teaching my daughters how to be successful when they have families of their own.

Now, when I wake up in the morning, I have a clear purpose—a defined "why." I approach each day with tenacious determination and energy because I know that if I give my all to whatever I'm doing, it will translate into success for my family. My "why" will be fulfilled.

Your "why" can be whatever you want it to be. Find that one thing that will motivate you to push forward every day. Whatever it may be, make sure your "why" will be a constant reminder of your ultimate goal. Write it on a sticky note, and put it on your bathroom mirror or the dash in your car. If you've had an awesome day, look at your "why" and feel good that you're one step closer to achieving it. If you've had a bad day, look at your "why" and realize that tomorrow is a new day with new challenges, and you'll meet them head-on and push forward.

Sometimes finding your "why" isn't as easy as having an "aha" moment at the dinner table. So, here are some steps that can help you define your "why."

Step One: Think about your dreams. If time, skill, and money were no object, and you could write your own story, what would it look like? For example, the image I have is my family and me traveling the world and experiencing different cultures.

Step Two: Take that image of your dreams and figure out where you financially need to be to make it a reality. Do you need to make a certain amount of money personally? Do you need to create an organization and raise enough funds for your group to accomplish its goals? What do you need to do to fund your dream?

Step Three: Come up with an action plan—a clear, concise plan to reach your goal and fulfill your "why." Where will you be a month from now, six months from now, a year from now, five years from now? Start out with small steps, don't overwhelm yourself at the beginning. A steady pace with consistent effort will get you farther than running one hundred miles an hour for a few days and coming to a stop, only to run hard again later and stop. Remember the old tale of the tortoise and the hare? Write down your action plan and follow it.

Step Four: Think about the challenges you will face and how to overcome them. I don't know of a single successful person who has never met with bumps on the road to achieving their goals. It's going to happen, but do not let those bumps steer you off your path. Plan for challenges, know how you'll tackle them, and move forward.

Step Five: Have a support system. It may be your family, your friends, or a mentor who shares similar goals or has a similar "why" as you. Lean on them for support and give them the support they need. It's much easier to succeed in fulfilling your "why" when you have support. It's not fun feeling like you're on an island by yourself. Make sure you have people on the island with you striving for the same success.

Step Six: When you have the first five steps in place and take action, the last step is easy. Enjoy your success, knowing you gave your best, consistent effort towards your "why" and that it's now a reality. You did it!

The last thing I encourage everyone to do is this: Once you have accomplished your "why," come up with another one. Never stop reaching for something great. Idle minds are the devil's playground. If you have a servant's heart, share your success with others. Help them find their "why." Imagine how wonderful you will feel knowing you have reached your goals, and now, you're helping others do the same.

I truly believe that we are all given the ability for greatness. However, ability does not always create greatness. Find your "why," plan how you will achieve it, and execute. Use your God-given abilities, and you will accomplish your "why."

My hope is that my story has touched you in some way. If nothing else, I hope you take this one thing away from it. You will always be a success if you have a "why."

BIOGRAPHY

Matt Sharpe is a graduate of North Carolina State University with a degree in business management. He has two decades of experience in B2B sales, B2C sales, and direct marketing. Matt currently runs a successful direct marketing business while also working with a multi-state equipment dealership as a territory manager. From Matt's humble beginnings in rural North Carolina, he has achieved his goals of success while remembering the wholesome values instilled in him by his parents. He believes everyone is put on this earth with the ability for greatness. His mission is to mentor as many people as possible to achieve success through positive leadership. He currently resides in Four Oaks, North Carolina, with his wife of twenty years, Lori, and his two daughters, Chloe and Sadie.

Connect with Matt Sharpe via https://linktr.ee/mattsharpe92

CHAPTER 23

PHOENIX

By Melissa Wade

I moved to California from Minnesota when I was twenty-three. School was behind me, and I had landed my first "real" job at a CPA firm. After a few years of working there and meeting business owners in every industry, I found myself staring out my office window and thinking, 'If they can do it, so can I!' There was nothing that made them more special, talented, or better than me. As a matter of fact, I was their accountant and wondered how some of them were even in business to begin with or how they had managed up to that point without going out of business because they weren't exactly what I would call the sharpest tools in the shed. After months of wondering what I should do, I got invited to a presentation at a hotel, and *that* is where I caught the vision—a vehicle to become self-employed. I signed up right on the spot, and ten weeks later, I had become a sales director and earned the use of my first free car.

I was a single mom with a two-year-old at the time. I longed to be home with my daughter. However, a single-income household didn't make it seem possible. The problem with the immediate success with my first experience in network marketing at the age of twenty-seven was that I didn't know how to build a solid foundation for my business. I didn't know how to lead others effectively. I really didn't have a working team or an organization with a solid foundation. Because of this, I was doing all the work. I was working 24/7. I was exhausted, discouraged, and I did not have more time with my daughter. It was not at all what I had imagined it to be or what I was told it would be like from the lady who recruited me. As if that wasn't frustrating enough, I found out I was pregnant. My boyfriend and I broke up, and I realized that I was going to be a single mom with two kids. My family was in the Midwest, and I felt completely alone. I fell into a deep depression, and that was the first time I quit.

When my son was one and my daughter five, I married a guy with three children. We definitely had our hands full with five kids, four of them under the age of six. With my experience working at the CPA firm, I started my own accounting practice. And because I love to do crafty things, I started a part-time gourmet gift basket business. My husband was self-employed in construction. Outside of a crazy schedule, everything was clicking along fine, then 2008 happened. The stock market crashed, the housing market fell, and businesses were going under. My husband's construction business flatlined, gift basket orders dried up, and my accounting clients were in trouble, and therefore, could not pay me for the work I had already done, nor could they keep me on. Like so many other families, our house went into foreclosure. It was the first time I laid in bed awake at night, wondering how we were going to keep the lights on and wondering how we were going to put food on the table. I woke up one day and thought that there was no way this could get any worse. I couldn't see a way out, so I decided to give network marketing another try. And this time, quitting and failure wasn't even an option. I called the gal who recruited me the first time and told her I was ready to hit the ground running.

I rose to the company's top ranks, drove a free car, earned diamonds, and spoke on stage. The house was no longer in foreclosure, and I was excited at the thought of having a prosperous future. Because failure was not an option. What was missing, though? My purpose and passion. Even though I was experiencing success, there was something not sitting right with me: the "fake it till you make it," the "we are not here to do anything other than selling the dream" trainings for the "top 2 percent," and the "dress for success" attitude of women who spent more money than they could afford to look like a million bucks. Some of them couldn't pay their electric bill, but they had no problem throwing another pair of designer shoes on a credit card, hoping to attract the person that would make their "month." Or even worse, some were racking up astronomical debt to finish whatever goal they had (to keep their position of leadership, to keep their "free" car, or simply to appear to be more successful than they really were). I can't tell you how many times I heard, 'I just need one solid month to pay off this debt and get to even.' Sadly, most of them always chased that "solid month" month after month, year after year.

You see, my passion is helping people, and after almost ten years, it became obvious to me that nothing I was doing was helping anyone other than myself (maybe?), my upline, and the company. I called the company and told them to come and pick up their car. I was done. I couldn't look myself in the mirror and feel good about "helping others" when it was all just smoke in mirrors. I was burnt out. I was exhausted. I was working seven days a week. I was overweight. I was a stranger to my family. I was depressed. And I felt like a complete and utter failure. That was the second time I quit.

Over the next few years, I joined several network marketing companies, many of them "ground-level opportunities" that went nowhere, except to put me further and further in debt just trying to survive. Needless to say, I was discouraged, disheartened, and completely turned off by the idea of network marketing. I had seen it ALL. It was then that I decided to fuel my passion for helping others and start my own online boutique. I had a customer base, the gift of gab, relationships with vendors in Los Angeles in the fashion district, and a good eye for fashion. Also, it was something I could do from home. I was able to connect with my customers and help them feel beautiful and confident, no matter their size. It felt amazing to help build an online community that focused not just on fashion but lifestyle and community. These women were not just customers; many became friends. The more I helped people, the more the community felt like a community, and the happier I was. But what I didn't realize was that I was not just building a support system for other women; I was building one for myself. After twelve years of marriage, I asked my husband to go to therapy. And when he refused, I asked for a divorce.

The divorce was a long time coming. It took the kids getting older and not needing so much time to free up, which led to a lot of inward reflection and observation. I married my then-husband just six months after we met. We were both single parents living in Southern California, where the cost of living is astronomical. I am not sure exactly when the marriage turned from 'I love you' to cohabitating out of necessity. But thinking back on it, it had been going on for a very long time. Adoration for me had turned into nit-picking about how I spent my time, belittling me, insulting my intelligence, criticizing my business, making me the butt of jokes with his children, trying to embarrass me in front of other people, telling the kids (and anyone who would listen) what a bad cook I was, banning me from the kitchen (even when cooking; I loved to cook), and I was always wondering what I'd be yelled at for next. I honestly think he thought I would never leave because, financially, it would have been nearly impossible. Plus, my family was still in the Midwest.

Within twenty-four hours of this happening, my mom called me to say they were selling their house in Minnesota and moving to Arizona to get ready for retirement. I was thrilled because I was starting to worry about my parents and the brutal winters. But before I could say anything else, I opened my mouth, and "me too" tumbled out. I told her about the divorce. And this is where the intentional designing of my life started. For the first time since I was younger, I actually felt like I could do or be whatever or whoever I wanted. I was genuinely excited about my future and about life. Isn't it amazing how what is perceived as the impossible, when it is the right thing for your life, will start lining up and unfolding just the way it is supposed to? Ralph Waldo Emerson said, "Once you make a decision, the universe conspires to make it happen,"[6] and I believe that 100 percent.

I would be lying if I said divorce was a walk in the park. It sucks. It sucks big time, and it's not until you are forced to lay everything out that you get the entire picture. My ex took out loans for over $1,000,000 to invest in a business in an industry he knew nothing about. Income taxes had not been paid for several years, and the credit cards were maxed out. Then Covid hit, and we were forced to quarantine together.

For the first time in my adult life, I had clarity. I had a goal and knew what I needed to do to make it happen, and I had a support system in my family and my online community. I was also able to start dreaming again, reconnecting with who I really am and what I'm passionate about. I started my journey of healing and discovery. Just before the pandemic, I completed my 200 RYT and became a yoga teacher, got certificates in laughter yoga and

6   "Ralph Waldo Emerson Quotes," BrainyQuote (Xplore), accessed October 11, 2021, https://www.brainyquote.com/quotes/ralph_waldo_emerson_383633.

kids' yoga! Becoming a yoga teacher was something I had wanted to do for fifteen years.

Moving to Phoenix was the best thing I could have ever done. This new chapter of my life has been everything I have wanted it to be. Instead of life and situations happening by default, I realized that I got a "do-over," and I could create the life I wanted—the life I dreamed of, that I never thought was possible.

I now have an amazing partner, and our relationship is built on trust, communication, and mutual respect. He has taught me so much about love and adventure, working hard but also playing hard, and that life wasn't meant to just get through; it was meant to be LIVED. During the pandemic, I completed a one-year full-time program becoming a Pilates instructor. I explored my passion for health and wellness *and* helping people.

I still have my online boutique/community. Without the support of strangers who became customers, then friends, I am not sure how I would have survived. The network marketing thing? My business is all on social media, and it's not uncommon for me to be approached several times a week with many different opportunities. After a while, I decided that I wasn't opposed to it. After all, I have met some of my closest friends as a result of it. However, it had to be the right opportunity, with the right products and the right company. And just like that, one of my girlfriends (whom I met years ago in a different network marketing company) called and said, "Girl, trust me. You have to check out what I'm doing." Once again, the universe answered. What she discovered and shared with me was exactly what I had been looking for: the highest quality products, a community on social media FULL of testimonials about how these products are changing lives and promoting a culture of health, wellness, positivity, and genuine care for others. Not only that, the income I am helping others earn is genuinely making a difference for families. THIS! *This* is what was missing. Be the energy you want to attract. Ask, and you shall receive. What you think about, you bring about.

BIOGRAPHY

Melissa Wade grew up in the Midwest and spent twenty years building several successful businesses in Los Angeles before relocating to Phoenix. An influencer having done hundreds of ads on YouTube, Facebook, TikTok, Instagram, and Amazon, she also runs an online group focused on fashion, body positivity, healthy lifestyle, and community. Melissa has been featured in several newspaper articles highlighting her businesses as well as online publications with VoyageLA. With her school report cards saying, "talks too much," Melissa turned her gift of gab into the ability to connect with and inspire others. Leading her teams to the top of several network marketing companies, she has traveled all over the country to train and speak on stage. She is a strong believer in dreaming big, the power of positive thinking, and celebrating small daily "wins" that lead to big successes. Melissa loves her family, dogs, and a good Netflix binge. On the weekends, she can be found off-roading, hiking, camping, and extreme adventuring. She lives out the quote by Robert Biswas-Diener, "I believe that living out loud and not letting fear hold you back is the key to the fullest, most rewarding life possible."

Connect with Melissa Wade via https://linktr.ee/MelissaKayWade

CHAPTER 24

NEVER QUIT AND KEEP PUSHING FOR YOUR GOALS

By Mihai Both

I was stuck in a moment, thinking about whether I deserved to be a part of this world. At that time, many things were happening that were not in my favour—nothing good was happening. I worked hard every day, and on certain days, I'd experience burnout and unhappiness.

When I was nine years old, my parents owned a little shop in the village. I remember them being very busy running that store, sometimes even missing out on days and nights with my brother and me. He and I would sometimes play around the shop just to be around them. We were raised mostly by our grandparents and an uncle and aunt. My uncle was an engineer, and my aunt was an accountant for a prestigious company. Both of them were my role models for achieving success.

I did not come from a family background of big business owners. This gave me the motivation to believe in my own abilities, not be a worker forever, and build the life I always wanted while staying well-connected with my family.

From a young age, we were taught to go to school, learn well, and become the best because that would lead to graduation, landing a well-paid job, and high status in the market. But I've never been one of the top students in school. I was somewhere around the middle—sometimes even lower than that. This excluded me from the rest of the college crowd. I was more focused on playing football, even though I was an amateur. However, I entertained the idea that this could be my way to fame, fortune, and a better lifestyle—being a football player. However, I was not very talented and never had a trainer who could take my career decision to the next level.

After I finished college, I needed to write an exam that would give me the opportunity to attend a university and study electrical engineering. I only chose that route because a few of my friends were doing the same, and I wanted to follow them. Of course, I also thought about making money at the same time and not having to depend on my parents' income for personal expenses. So, I began to look for ways to make money, preferably through a job that paid me a salary. I was hellbent on finding a job to make my own money because we were raised and taught that way: go to school, get a job, and keep working whether you like it or not.

I finished college with a technical skill under my belt, and of course, most employers told me the same thing: "You don't have enough experience yet, and we can't employ you." I got a job as an electrician in a company and worked there for almost two years. After a few years, I wanted to get more in terms of experience in life and sought to grow financially and make more money.

I went to work in Italy with a long-term plan in mind and wanted to build the life I wanted there. I had everything I wanted there for the first few weeks: good work and making decent money. For a young man like me, it was good enough to keep me motivated and focused enough to keep going day after day. The job was not easy. I worked for the construction industry, where one needed to put in hard work and have a powerful mindset day in and day out. We resided in a flat on the top story in Torino, where the winters got really cold. Both the construction site and our residence were cold. On some days, it was colder in the residence than it was outside. This was not the life I wanted to live. We didn't know when the apartment would get hot water for a warm shower or when the heaters would function.

It got to a point where I became very depressed because I was missing my family and friends. On top of that, living this poor lifestyle made me question if leaving them and making these sacrifices was even worth it. It felt as if I was stuck in this situation indefinitely. There was a battle between two thoughts in my mind: stay and keep working or leave this place and go back to my home country, Romania. I tried to motivate myself every day by telling myself, 'One more day. Just one more day.' After a few months of this internal struggle and being very unhappy, I found that the dream of changing my life was powerful enough to keep me going.

One day, I had a discussion with my boss about holidays. He came off as very ignorant and dismissive about my request to take Christmas off. I wanted to go back home to my family and friends for Christmas, and my boss did not have the money to pay our monthly wages. Fortunately, I had some savings, and I booked a one-way bus ticket from Italy to Romania, with no intention of coming back. I was back in Romania and got to spend the holidays with my family and friends. After the holidays, I went back to working for my old company in Romania and carried on with my journey from there.

A new chapter began, and I had to start from square one, just many other times in my life because I never had the passion for growing or taking things up a notch by taking a few risks. Throughout all the difficult situations and struggles I faced, I was motivated to take another step and do something different, but I just never knew how to go about it. I recognized that I was not proud of any of my past decisions and that they affected my relationship with my family, friends, and colleagues. This was because I would blame them for my inability to do well—I blamed everyone but myself.

I began to delve into personal development courses and started following successful people—people who started out with situations like mine (or worse) yet managed to find their way out of it. This helped me to better understand how things were going in my life and how nobody was going to give me my life's vision. My vision was about what *I* wanted to do in this world.

My vision—my dreams, beliefs, and mission—is about what I wanted to do for myself in my life. I realized that some people figure this out quickly while others need more time. What makes the process faster is being surrounded by like-minded people— those who have the same ideas and hobbies as you. You have to find people with whom you share a common point. That's going to create a connection between you and them, which will, in turn, make you grow and become a better version of yourself. Sometimes, it's other people who can see in you what you don't see in yourself. They give you the belief and trust necessary for you to see what you truly want and believe that you can get it done.

I have learned to always stand up for myself in any good or bad situation and try to learn what errors to avoid and what to do better next time. Every failure is a lesson, so there's no need to become frustrated with failures. Take failures with happiness, believe in yourself, and do not let anyone drag you away from your dreams. You are bound to run into people who do not believe in your goals. Sometimes, these can be family, friends, and people whom you deeply trust. They just won't see things from your perspective. They will probably want to "drag you back to reality." But your reality is yours, not theirs. If you have a dream, start to work on it. If you fail, learn from your mistakes and keep moving forward. Apply these lessons to your next idea and go ahead with full force.

I've always sought after something better—to have a better life and try different things. Doing this required a little bit more time and passion than I used to give in the past; I'd always want everything to go quickly, not taking into account my experiences in the given situation. At the end of the day, I cannot compare myself to anyone else because their knowledge, experience, current situation, and background story is most likely very different from my own.

I've learned to do things in my own time and believe in myself. I dream about becoming my own boss, working for myself, and building the life of my dreams.

You will find your path to success. Just believe.

BIOGRAPHY

Mihai Both is a self-made entrepreneur who owns an electrical and sales company. He is originally from Romania. Since 2015, he has been living with his family in the UK, where he runs his company. He loves his family and loves helping others.

Connect with Mihai Both via https://linktr.ee/Mihaiboth

CHAPTER 25

TO LIVE IS IN YOUR POWER

By Natalya Hramova

> "In the depth of winter, I finally learned that within me there lay an invincible summer."[7]
>
> —Albert Camus

Morning is longer than night—the morning when I decided to die.

As the deep night surrendered to the gray light of gloomy morning, I woke up to the nightmare of my life. I was in my forties, and it was the second month of what my therapist called "anxious depression." Whatever was happening to me, in my opinion, was only partially my fault. The monsters inside me were real; they were telling me that life was unfair, and I was destined to lose this battle.

A torrent of turbulent memories covered me like a heavy blanket, and I struggled to catch my breath. My inflamed brain

---

7   "A Quote by Albert Camus," Goodreads (Goodreads), accessed August 9, 2021, https://www.goodreads.com/quotes/2313-in-the-depth-of-winter-i-finally-learned-that-within.

showed me a grim slideshow of the bitter defeats I experienced during my so-called happy and relatively successful life. It looked like the person I knew—a gifted musician and journalist in Ukraine and an accomplished nurse in Canada—had hit rock bottom searching for meaning and failing to find it. All I wanted was to fall asleep and never wake up.

Most of my childhood memories were not very happy. I grew up with a lot of Musts, Shoulds, and Ought Tos. My parents loved me intensely but in their own way. My father was very kind, but his busy journalist's life did not let him participate much in the pedagogic drill. My mother was a strong, domineering woman, and her love towards me was despotic. It was a suffocating love: every step, every breath, even my every thought was scrutinized and controlled. Despite that, I loved her back, fearfully and anxiously, constantly trying to earn approval and kindness. Loneliness seemed to follow me wherever I went. Being fiercely bullied at school left me yearning for acceptance. I learned to blend in and love everyone unconditionally, all the while feeling inadequate, worthless, and completely isolated on the inside.

I remembered clearly how at the age of eleven, true anxiety entered my life. I woke up in the middle of the night, short of breath and sweaty, with the sudden realization that I was afraid to live. Everything that life would hold for me seemed terrifying and unkind. This fear was so real that it left a sticky, nauseating taste in my mouth—a taste I came to be all too familiar with.

I always had very high expectations for myself. My parents, on the other hand, did not, once telling me that while my brother was genuinely brilliant, I was "simply kind." Being simply kind was not enough for me, however. I needed to be intelligent, inventive, successful, and independent. So, I fought hard. I fought for everything: top marks at my first university, applause after playing a musical recital in front of a big audience, and praise for the articles and interviews I wrote. I fought for all of these things with an ever-present taste of fear on the tongue and a bitter realization that no matter how much I achieved, I was not enough. This pattern of extreme fear followed me around like my shadow: every win, every achievement, and every obstacle overcome was paired with a fear of failure and rejection.

My first panic attack came, insidiously, on the day of my arrival in Canada. As our plane landed, crushing pain and terror engulfed me and carried me into a world of darkness. The uncertainty, loneliness, and feeling of complete disconnection from reality in the aftermath left me devasted, terrified, and guilty. It was the first time I perceived death as salvation. Though these dark, threatening thoughts filled my head, as the plane's landing gear touched the tarmac, I reminded myself that I had an unemployed husband to support, a seven-year-old child to raise, and a fresh, unpredictable life in a new country to build. I told myself to get over my fear and carried on with a heavy heart.

I was twenty-eight when I swallowed my first anti anxiety medication. Many followed until I lost track. Bandaids on a deep wound, the pills were a stopgap, allowing me to function without healing the hurt. Despite my fears, I continued to seemingly succeed in whatever I attempted, but my wounds continued to bleed. Even with an ever-changing regimen of medication and long therapy sessions, there were dozens of panic attacks. They would last for long hours, sometimes days, and they got me admitted to the hospital twice. After being heavily medicated and haphazardly fixed, I would be discharged and sent back to my personal hell.

Eventually, my fear and the panic that walked in lockstep with it took control of my life. I would say no to exciting trips, avoid parties, and would not even pick up the telephone because I was scared to hear bad news. My bedroom became my shelter, a place where I could hide from the world and curse my fate, wallowing in my misery. Deep down, however, I came to suspect that the reason for my suffering was lodged somewhere inside of me. If only I could find it and draw it out.

I always knew that I wanted to help people, and in a search for meaning, I decided that responding to this desire would bring me some sense of peace. Soon after came the idea of becoming a nurse, and as I started studying, I discovered that nursing was my true calling. Graduating from nursing school with honors, I quickly built the career of my wildest dreams: being accepted into the province's most acute intensive care unit, where I felt powerful and accomplished. This feeling lasted until my first death experience, which shattered my carefully constructed illusion of control. As the years went by, my sense of helplessness grew day by day: no matter how much I tried to save many patients, they would be gone forever. My inability to preserve life shook me so profoundly that I had to leave the ICU. Nevertheless, wherever I went, I was followed by the same sense of defeat and a persistent feeling of guilt.

As I lay in my bed, I knew that I was both a prisoner and my own cruel jailer. My soul was lost and aching, and the internal monologues did not bring any clarity. I asked myself a million questions. The main question was, "Why?" Why did I have to suffer so much? Was I destined to die from fear and helplessness every time I attempted to live fully? Was this God's plan for me? I always wanted to believe in His divine guidance, that He would give me a much-needed relief after my many trials. But relief did not come. Instead, I found myself in the depth of despair, guilt, and worthlessness, only wishing to die. An unavoidable answer popped into my head: "God does not love you; you are not deserving."

The darkest memory of my life visited me that day. England, 1995. I, a Ukrainian student, picked strawberries on an English farm in the hope of collecting the money needed for immigration to Canada. Sixty young men and only six women were on the farm, working sixteen hours in the fields and earning three English pounds per hour. When night fell, exhausted from the hard physical labor, we would retreat into tiny trailers where we would collapse on old and uncomfortable beds. One night I woke up from a struggle: I was not alone in my bed. I felt a firm palm on my mouth, and a scream for help was stuck in my throat. That night I lost. Since then, I started to truly hate myself.

In your darkest place and your darkest hour, life has a mysterious ability to send you surprises. Some people recount stories of angels or their human ancestors that come to relay a sacred message. For me, it happened to be my mother. When I was sixteen, she kept repeating that I needed to be my best self and aim for the very top. I never paid much attention to those educational drills as a teenager and even recalling them as an adult. The only answer I could muster was: "I am deep down, mom! I am vulnerable and fearful! I am broken." The morning I decided to die, I wept and asked my deceased mom for forgiveness for what I was planning. Suddenly, her usually firm and demanding voice softened and said, "There is a purpose to this pain, my girl. You *will* rise up. Again and again. The road will be mastered by the one walking."

Overcoming. The gift that life presented me and that I had been ignoring for decades. As I started contemplating the words of encouragement that I had just heard, I was hit with a sudden epiphany: life was happening not *to* me, but *for* me. Life was happening *for* me so that I could continue to learn and grow, so that my spirit could mature, and that my character could be fortified like tempered steel. Grit. That's the gift that my mother gave me. Back home, we call it a *sterzhen*, a metal rod that holds you together when you are close to falling apart.

But there also was kindness. "You are simply kind," my parents told me. I know I shared my most profound empathy with many people around me. But was I kind to myself? Not at all.

Eventually, I realized that the only way to survive the madness of my affair with fear was to learn how to be kind to my inner child. I started conversing with the frightened little girl I had hiding inside me and listening to the revelations she had to share.

With newly born self-kindness, acceptance slowly entered my life. I accepted my numerous flaws and my failures. I realized that I had the right to be lost and that it was okay to make even the biggest mistakes in life. That I could not save every patient on this earth. I welcomed fear as a part of my life. I befriended it and listened to it, and as I opened up to it, it stopped controlling me.

I can undoubtedly say that what I considered to be my failures—fear and anxiety—have taught me to connect with my soul, a connection that was missing but crucial to me leading a meaningful and courageous life. For most of my teenage and adult years, I was completely disconnected from my deepest core, failing to truly listen to my fear and what it was trying to tell me. I struggled to be accepted at any cost, trading my authenticity for the love of others. All of my internal conflicts and contradictions remained unresolved until I fully surrendered to and accepted them. Step-by-step, I had to address each wound and fear and learn why they had a place in my journey. As Edgar Allan Poe once said, "Never to suffer would never to have been blessed."[8] Sinking deep into darkness had brought an unexpected light into my life and shaped me into a better, kinder person, capable of accepting my flaws alongside my virtues.

Sometimes you have to dive and reach the very bottom to float to the surface. My life still has some rough waters, and I am an imperfect captain of an imperfect ship. But I know now that I have the privilege of finding and becoming who I was meant to be. I practice forgiveness, kindness, and strength with my whole

---

8   "A Quote by Edgar Allan Poe," Goodreads (Goodreads), accessed August 9, 2021, https://www.goodreads.com/quotes/40870-never-to-suffer-would-never-to-have-been-blessed.

heart and soul. My mess has become my message, and I share it with you now: when you accept yourself for who you are, it makes you not only compassionate but strong as well. It does not make you perfect, and there are pages of your life yet to be written with future victories and losses. You will fall and rise again and repeat this cycle many times on your path. But by choosing to walk, you will give your wounds a chance to heal. You will come to know your purpose and be true to yourself. This will give you incredible power—the power to live.

BIOGRAPHY

At first glance, professional musician, journalist, nurse, and entrepreneur, Natalya Hramova seems to be an amalgam of incompatibilities. The author of multiple art-related articles and interviews published in Ukraine, Natalya's most recent work focuses on the human soul's struggle. Immigration to Canada has not stopped her from doing what she has always loved— writing while daily caring for patients in one of Canada's most prominent hospitals. "In a world where you can be anything, be kind" is her favorite motto, and as a mental health advocate, her compassionate care has touched the lives of many. She continues to inspire not only her patients but also her team members and friends to be their best selves while facing adversity with courage.

Connect with Natalya Hramova via
https://linktr.ee/Natalya_Hramova

CHAPTER 26

ADVERSITY NEVER SLEEPS

By Patti Culver

I was only ten years old when I first realized that life wasn't perfect. I'd been sent to my room by my mom because she didn't want my sister or me to hear the ugliness that would ensue in our living room. I could hear my mother's tearful pleas and my father's occasional comments. When we were finally summoned to the living room, we were seated and told my parents were getting a divorce. I was devastated. Soon after that, my father quietly retreated to the bedroom, grabbed the pillow he would be taking with him, and quietly left the house.

That scenario took place over fifty years ago, but it is still fresh in my mind, as are my other traumatic life experiences. But somehow, I got through them. Was it sheer will, a resilient personality, or grace? I really don't know. Perhaps it was a combination of all. What I do know is that the human spirit has no limitations on healing, provided the soul is fed and given proper care. But it would take me many years and many trials to finally figure this out.

Waitress, wildland firefighter, secretary: these are just a few of the many and varied occupations I've had over the years. But I finally decided to train as a legal assistant. After schooling, I started my first job, working for an attorney at age twenty-one. Through the next twenty years, I had several legal and administrative jobs, the last being a Grants Coordinator/Housing Specialist at a municipality in Central California. I had to drag myself out of bed each morning to face another day of working an unfulfilling office job. Even though it sucked the life out of my soul, I couldn't complain; it paid the bills. I *lived* for each vacation day I could take. That year, I was particularly excited.

After a wonderful, extended camping trip in the Sierra mountains of California in July 2000, I felt myself getting sick with what I thought was the flu. My joints and muscles were in a great deal of pain, and I had a fever and typical flu symptoms. After about ten days, the flu symptoms began to subside. Little did I know, my illness was just beginning. In addition to the joint pain, I started developing cognitive problems and severe depression. I was nauseated all the time, and I literally could not get out of bed. This prompted me to seek medical treatment from my primary care doctor. But as it turned out, he had absolutely *no* clue as to what was causing this mysterious illness.

After consulting with over twenty doctors, including a psychiatrist who told me, "Pull yourself up by your bootstraps and carry on," I was still without answers. I was so ill that I had to quit my job, which was devastating because most of my friends were from work. So, I found myself jobless, friendless, and sicker than I had ever been in my life.

Luckily, someone referred me to an endocrinologist in the early part of 2001. He was an odd but brilliant man, and he performed a litany of physical and lab tests. He found that I had many abnormalities with my thyroid, and I ultimately underwent a thyroid gland biopsy. I waited three grueling weeks before I got a definitive answer.

CANCER. No word in any language strikes you with more fear. I was immediately scheduled for a total thyroidectomy, which took place within a few weeks of my diagnosis. They found that I had mixed papillary/follicular carcinoma of the thyroid gland. When I woke up, I discovered I had a five-inch incision across the base of my throat. I thought I looked like a modern-day Frankenstein. Even though I had physical evidence of surgery, I still had a difficult time wrapping my head around the fact that I had cancer. What would happen now? What about my kids and my husband? Would I live a long life, or would I succumb to this dreaded disease?

After a few weeks of recovery from my surgery, I got a PET scan, which illuminated the areas where the cancer was still existent. My endocrinologist and surgeon explained that I would have to undergo radioactive iodine radiation therapy. This is a bizarre treatment where you swallow radioactive pills that seek out and destroy active thyroid cancer cells within your body. I was sequestered in a special room at the hospital, with no human contact, with plastic covering all surfaces, including the phone and the toilet. Speaking of toilets, I'll spare you the details of the joys of radioactive pee.

After three days, I was allowed to go home to my family, but I had to stay 15 feet away from them for another ten days. Just when I needed hugs the most, I couldn't have them. It was a particularly overwhelming and lonely time for me, and I did a lot of soul-searching. It was just me, the TV, and countless episodes of sitcom reruns. The radiation treatment made me indescribably ill, although I was healing from the surgery. I rallied and actually started feeling a little better after a few weeks. I thought I was on my way to recovery, putting all this behind me and going on with my life. But my original illness began making me violently sick again, and the search for my underlying disease began all over. It was like a nightmare from which I couldn't wake up!

After two more years of continued illness and consulting with even more physicians, I was still not diagnosed with a particular systemic illness, nor was I getting any better. After further follow-up testing, I was recommended to undergo another round of RAI radiation therapy. There were still cancer cells lurking in my body, and they needed to be eradicated. Once again, I had radiation sickness, on top of my existing mystery illness, and I thought I would never feel well again. This time, I thought I would finally be healed. But it was not to be.

In 2003, my husband and I had the great fortune of moving to the great state of Utah. We quickly settled into our new home, and I loved my new life here, despite my continued physical problems. I got established with some new doctors, including a wonderful endocrinologist who eventually became a trusted friend. After following me for a few years, a routine lab test revealed that my tumor marker was once again high. This prompted another PET scan, and it revealed the cancer had now spread to the lymph nodes on the right side of my neck. I couldn't believe it! Why God? Why was this happening?

After meeting with an amazing head and neck surgeon, it was determined that I would undergo lymph node removal on the right side of my neck to prevent the cancer from spreading to other organs. The surgery went smoothly, and after a bout of frozen shoulder due to my position on the operating table, I began to heal quickly. Unfortunately, I was required to undergo a third round of RAI radiation, and this time, I was sicker than ever before. I renewed my search for the underlying illness when the worst of the radiation illness was over. My search took me to places, physically and emotionally, where I had never been before. But this time, things would start to change.

In 2006, I had an eye infection that required me to see a specialist. As it turned out, this particular eye problem was only seen in elderly patients with long-term autoimmune disease and people with Lyme disease. LYME DISEASE? I'd heard about that illness in passing, and I never really paid much attention to it. But this mention of Lyme being a possible link to my eye problem set me out on a new investigation. I scoured the internet, reading everything I could about this bizarre and misunderstood disease. What I learned was that there were over twenty symptoms, and I had EVERY. SINGLE. ONE.

Based on my research, I convinced my primary care doctor to order a new, special test for Lyme disease for people who had chronic illnesses. At the time, Lyme disease was quite controversial in medical and political circles, so I was lucky my doctor complied. When the results came back, I felt like I had just won an Olympic event; I was highly positive for Lyme disease!

Though I had just been diagnosed with a horrendous, life-changing disease, I was exuberant. After seven long years of severe illness and being told it was 'all in my head,' I finally had the answer I was looking for. Now, the search for a Lyme-literate physician ensued. Luckily, I found a naturopathic physician specializing in Lyme disease treatment in Provo, Utah, just four hours away from home.

My doctor was magnificent! She treated me with prescription antibiotics, herbs, and supplements. And though it wasn't easy, and I was still extremely ill, the dark clouds began to part, and I could finally begin to see glimpses of light in my life. It would be almost three years of treatment until I was finally at a point when I was feeling better (finally!) and at a point of Lyme remission. I credit my eye doctor and my Lyme doctor for literally saving my life. And I continue to see both of them to this day to help manage my health. As it turns out, my cancer was just an "incidental" finding, and Lyme was the underlying illness all of these years.

Though I'm still not in perfect health, and I'll continue to have lingering symptoms for the rest of my life, I'm cancer-free at this point, and I haven't had a Lyme flare for at least a year.

Having gone through all of this, I consider myself lucky: lucky my cancer didn't spread to other organs, lucky I was able to manage my chronic Lyme and preserve my life.

Even in the darkest days, there is light. And it is this light that keeps us going. Even though I underwent tremendous illness and pain, there were blessings that came out of my experiences. My cancer caused me to re-examine my work and what I was doing with my life, and once again, I got reacquainted with God. I even found my religion and a newfound faith in things seen and unseen. I found the acts of gratitude and humility, and I surrendered my circumstances to a power greater than myself. It was in this surrender that I found my strength.

Am I telling you I'm happy I had cancer and Lyme disease? Of course not! But I am saying that there is something to be learned even through the darkest of times, even if it's just to relate to someone else going through the same things. I believe God uses us to help each other, and I have consulted with many people who have undergone what I have, and I believe I have helped them. Was that why I had these illnesses? In many ways, I also learned many things along my journey, including how to be true to myself and my own wants, needs, and desires.

I concluded that I was so miserable in my occupation because I wasn't fulfilling my true calling on this planet. So, when I finally recovered from my illnesses, I set out to find what the calling really was. I discovered that I was meant to be here to help others in any way that I could.

That's why I chose network marketing as my new profession. I get to stay home and work or work in the Grand Tetons of Wyoming. I get to feel connected to others and help them with their health and finances. In this profession, you also grow as a human through personal development and fellowship with others on the same path. I am constantly learning and growing, and I've never felt happier. I'm directing my own path with help from God. And at sixty-three, I'm enjoying a level of fulfillment I never thought was possible in my working life.

It's a given: if you're human, you *will* experience trials and adversity. But it's what we do with that adversity that determines our destiny. Just look to something outside yourself for strength, whether it's God, a tree, or serendipity. Persevere, and you will find your way back to happiness.

I am eternally grateful to Matt Morris for giving me this opportunity to tell my story. He is a tremendous mentor, coach, and all-around human. He has given me skills, gumption, and courage. And if you don't know what gumption is, take a trip to Texas.

BIOGRAPHY

Patti Culver is a network marketing professional and co-author of *Breakthrough Leadership* by best-selling author Matt Morris. Patti has had a lifetime of personal and medical trials and challenges. She believes others can relate and that we all help each other heal and overcome adversity through our shared experiences. Patti began writing as a young girl and finished her last J.O.B. as a local government grant writer. She's an avid volunteer in her community. Patti lives and works out of her home amongst the beautiful red rock vistas of southwest Utah, where she resides with her husband, Jim. Her children and grandchildren are the focus of her life. She loves to travel and camp in her RV, is an avowed "gem geek," and enjoys watching motocross and air shows. Patti's favorite quote is one by George Eliot: "It's never too late to be what you might have been."

Connect with Patti Culver via https://linktr.ee/pattimelt7

CHAPTER 27

HARNESS THE POWER OF STORY

By Sa Huynh

In the life of a warrior, there are rhythms of fulfillment and disappointment. Japanese samurai, Miyamoto Musashi, writes of the rhythms that exist in everything:

"In the field of commerce, there are rhythms of becoming rich and losing one's fortune . . . If you do not understand these rhythms, your artistry will not be reliable . . . To win a battle is to know the rhythms of specific opponents, use rhythms that your opponents do not expect, and produce formless rhythms from rhythms of wisdom."[9]

Tahir Shah in Arabian Nights once said, "Stories are a communal currency of humanity."[10] Stories have helped me navigate the peaks and valleys of the mountains I have chosen

---

9   Musashi Miyamoto, "Chapter 1.8: The Earth Scroll / On Rhythm in Martial Arts," in *The Book of Five Rings: A Classic Text on the Japanese Way of the Sword*, trans. Thomas Cleary (Shambhala, 2005), pp. 20-21.

10 "A Quote from In Arabian Nights," Goodreads (Goodreads), accessed August 19, 2021, https://www.goodreads.com/quotes/532264-stories-are-a-communal-currency-of-humanity.

to embark. This is a tale from which I emerged, from a husk of timidity to the journey of an entrepreneurial warrior.

As a young girl, I wrote stories that catered to my imagination. Most notably, my favorite was about the jelly monster who lived in the sewer, snacking on my peanut butter sandwiches. This story allowed me to bond with the neighborhood kids from all walks of life. My friend, The Editor, whipped out her trusted red pen and bled over my rough drafts with notes in the margins, but HEY . . . I was delighted to have an audience!

Every weekend, my siblings and I were excited when dad dropped us off at the public library. We spent hours perusing the shelves, diving into all sorts of imaginative worlds. We were curious about a myriad of topics: economics, spirituality, law, fashion, vampires, patents, global affairs, manga, etc. The librarians offered several recommendations when we participated in annual summer reading clubs. Volunteers shared with us their love of snakes, backgammon, horror, and Polynesian dancing.

Adventuring the world quenched my burning curiosity. The food that I read about suddenly satiated my taste buds. The opera singer's ethereal voice in Bel Canto came to life when I listened to the Metropolitan Opera Night Stream. When I visited Vietnam with mom for the first time, the pace of life in the Quy Nhon countryside felt more languid than the bustling city life in Texas. My perception of time itself seemed to shift. The coastline induced a relaxed atmosphere. I relished the beauty of Da Lat, Nha Trang, and the Sapa Mountains.

Little did my parents know that this vacation relieved my mental anguish from a traumatic experience and the overall stress I experienced as a young adult. Years following my return to the states, I attended a family reunion. It was a beautiful summer afternoon. I munched on an egg roll and enjoyed the company of my lively family members as they shared their current pursuits and lessons from the past.

At the time, I wore a happy mask that concealed a dark black hole of loneliness. Consumed with depression, I lacked direction in an uncertain world. I dropped out of a college I loved with no degree in sight and drowned in recurring nightmares and panic attacks. Despite reaching out to friends and family for help, I struggled against the gravity of my anger and grappled with the concept of forgiving saboteurs. The housing market crash of 2007 impacted several Americans. The political climate on campus was volatile. I felt like I let my family down, and most of all, I felt like I let myself down. Self-doubt began to creep in like the plague and latched onto any exposed vulnerability I had failed to protect. My fragile identity and confidence shattered into millions of jagged pieces. Who am I?

I had an idyllic childhood in a peaceful Texan suburb filled with fond memories of water gun fights, Easter egg hunts, and baseball in the streets. With the help of a nurturing environment, I blossomed. My teachers expanded my horizons of what could be possible and told me that I could be anything. What happened to me? Did I just allow others and external events to stomp out my flame and extinguish my dreams?

Throughout high school, I earned academic achievements in electronics technology, physics, mathematics, and English. I studied circuit schematics to create cool things like an AM/FM radio and a remote-controlled race car. Web development, animation, and programming Lego robots brought me joy. Scholarships, grants, and graduating in the top ten percent paved the way toward the university's entrance. I majored in English literature, though I had plans of eventually transferring to an electrical engineering track. The future was looking bright and filled with promise.

Yet, for many years, I worked a semi-invisible role as a cashier, serving the public in retail. I felt like I lagged behind my peers in many ways. However, being out of the limelight allowed me to intimately connect with customers who confided in me about their own struggles. Sometimes, folks questioned why I was there. *"Shouldn't you be working at NASA? The police department? The hospital? The nail salon?"*

I was an exhausted knight, low on resources and battling an overwhelming number of monsters who regularly challenged my self-worth and tore holes into my armor. I missed the friendly jelly monster from my youth! Discovering fulfillment while being locked down in a cage was a challenge. Where was the key? Where in the world was the famed Holy Grail? How was I going to get there?

I sought help despite the stigma of the culture in which I was raised, wherein many remain silent about their woes, trials, and tribulations. I prayed at odd times of the day. My psychiatrist gave me his book as a gift. Within the chapter, "An Emergency Call," he shared an insight that struck me.

". . . after a traumatic experience, when the individual is recuperating, he can reorder his priorities and now the most important thing for him is to do things to improve his health and do altruistic deeds. When a person learns the 'hidden' messages of these 'negative' experiences, he wakes up, reorders his life, rearranges his values and for the first time, finds the meaning of what he does, of his interpersonal relationships, of life itself and he lives with greater intensity."[11]

To alleviate some of my personal suffering, I turned to service and theatre. I volunteered for health fairs and tutoring centers. I enjoyed seeing the students' eyes light up when they finally understood key ideas. I collected supplies for hurricane victims, the homeless, and domestic violence victims. I embraced network marketing to serve my community and their personal needs for connection.

---

11 Ramon Cuencas-Zamora, "Chapter 1: The Consequences of Work Stress / Section 6: An Emergency Call," in Doing Your Work with Love by Recovering Your Spirituality: Practical Strategies for Finding Your Mission in Life, 2008, p. 25.

Theatre allowed me to enter the mind of another character and put some distance between me and my thoughts. When reciting the lines for the role of a clown in the Shakespeare play, *Much Ado About Nothing*, I asked myself if I was just taking myself far too seriously and needed to lighten up a little. Once the play was over, though, I was forced to confront myself, which, according to Maya Angelou, required courage. I did not have to look far when I sought courageous role models. Courage and perseverance in the face of extreme adversity run in my family.

My uncle shared with me a story of his early days as a soldier. He was going about his day when suddenly, he was shot in the back. Doctors informed him that he was paralyzed from the neck down and that he would never walk again. Despite the grim prognosis, my uncle willed himself to think otherwise, against all odds.

Miraculously, he slowly wiggled his fingers and his toes. Eventually, he began to walk again! President Ronald Reagan gave him a medal, recognizing him for his courage. That day, my uncle taught me the importance of a powerful mindset, positive affirmations, and how it can overcome many obstacles.

My parents left Vietnam during the height of the communist invasion. My father was a maverick and left home in search of a more prosperous life while his siblings stayed behind. His parents were hardworking farmers who worked in the rice fields all day, bartering and trading in the outdoor markets just to make ends meet. College was nothing but a pipe dream for them.

Was dad scared to leave all he knew for something unknown? You bet he was! However, he was confident in his ability to discover a better life elsewhere. Dad traveled and lived in Hong Kong, California, and New York before he finally settled in Texas, where he met mom.

Mom witnessed her dad experience excruciating pain when a communist soldier forced him to kneel on the spiky shell of a durian fruit. One night, despite my mom's fearful trembling, grandma encouraged her to leave for America: "You are still young enough to be able to survive the journey. You have your whole life ahead of you, and it will be better there."

My mother and her siblings left in the middle of the night. Gunshots grazed their heads as they ducked in the boat floating down the river. History refers to them as the "Vietnamese Boat People" in the mass exodus that became one of the largest migrations and humanitarian crises following the Vietnam War.

My relatives survived a perilous trek where thousands died of dehydration, starvation, and piracy. My haggard parents arrived in America as refugees with nothing aside from the support of their family members. Back in Vietnam, the right to education was stripped away from the people and was reserved for the rich elite.

My parents knew its precious value and pursued their educational interests with vigor. A linguist worked with my father to teach him English and signed his workbook, "Never forget the power of words. Use them wisely." My mother learned English from volunteers at a local church. My dad later became a mechanic for airplanes, and my mom worked as a seamstress and later studied to become a cosmetologist.

How can the stories of my relatives empower my life? I tapped into an abundant stream that replenished me. Their inspirational stories reinvigorated my passion for life, knocked me out of the doldrums, and got me back in the ring to fight for the life I wanted to create.

I wiped away my tears, dusted my boots, rolled up my sleeves, and got to work. I re-enrolled myself back into college. I graduated with a degree in information technology and went on to pursue a master's program. I persistently searched for jobs in an incredibly competitive market, submitted hundreds of applications, and faced rejection after rejection. Every time a door slammed in my face, I asked myself a series of questions of what more I could do to prove myself worthy.

What kind of questions did I need to be asking to effectively learn from this experience and move closer to my goals? How could I improve the interview process? How could I further refine and polish my skills? What events could I attend that will enrich my life? What additional certifications did I need to study and earn? What kind of people did I need to connect with? What other experiences did I need? What kind of conversations did I need to be engaging in to move up to the next level? How did someone else get there?

Victory tasted so sweet when I finally landed my current role as a technical writer for a cybersecurity and software development firm. I was also blessed by the people I met along my business journey. The journey for growth is ongoing. In fact, a coworker has invited me to a flying lesson where I can soar like the eagles above! There are always new people to meet and new places to explore.

Richard Bach's book echoes within my mind. Jonathan Livingston Seagull delivers a moment of clarity, "Don't believe what your eyes are telling you. All they show is limitation. Look with your understanding. Find out what you already know, and you will see the way to fly."[12] A resilient warrior undergoes constant evolution to cast a vision into uncharted territory and win one of the most difficult battles of all: the war in one's mind.

---

12 "A Quote from Jonathan Livingston Seagull," Goodreads (Goodreads), accessed August 19, 2021, https://www.goodreads.com/quotes/11668-don-t-believe-what-your-eyes-are-telling-you-all-they.

BIOGRAPHY

Emboldened by stories that have been passed down by her family members, Sa Huynh is known for her determination and commitment to service. She is a tech writer at a cybersecurity firm. Sa earned a bachelor's degree in information technology and English literature. She has helped clients reach their career objectives by editing their resumes and creating documentation to enhance their businesses. She enjoys consulting clients on their skincare and nutritional needs. She volunteers with her local Rotary Club and was a recipient of the Paul Harris Fellow Award. Sa transports her readers to a variety of worlds on her blog by sharing poems, micro tales, inspirational quotes, and photos of her adventures.

Connect with Sa Huynh via https://linktr.ee/SunnySa

CHAPTER 28

FROM F.A.I.T.H. WITH G.O.D. WE L.E.A.D.

By Shane Adams

The spiritual side of leadership from which I come, in this context, is aimed at giving you a simple yet profound concept of my interpretation of what it means to lead yourself and others in a way that uplifts the spirit.

Let's begin with my concept of faith. It is the foresight of ascendant intelligence that transcends the heart (F.A.I.T.H.), meaning we are looking for guidance from a higher power with the gift of oneness from the divine (G.O.D.)—that we are all unified together, and as such, are all-powerful, both as one and as a whole, through divinity being the ultimate presence, however, you view this.

So, therefore, taking this into account, our purpose as leaders is to love, encourage, and acknowledge others' desires and drives (L.E.A.D.) that are sometimes similar but often different from our own. The best leaders do this powerfully!

Often, to love, encourage and acknowledge the drives and desires of others is to expect results and success to happen with an intended purpose (L.E.A.D.E.R.S.H.I.P.). It requires introspection necessary to find the leader within who unites, encourages, and networks to create an empire (I.N.F.L.U.E.N.C.E.).

I have learned these traits and values from watching great leaders and through my experience and gift of expression I received from a higher power.

When starting an endeavour or venture, it is crucial to begin with the end in mind, to lead with integrity, and engage with people and the process while having faith with grace. The results will be ongoing, and you will win by having a servant heart (B.E.L.I.E.F. G.R.O.W.S.).

I once heard that enthusiasm means enthus (God within) and iasm (I am sold myself). When you see it from that perspective, it is so powerful!

Acronyms, which, as you can see, I'm using here, are my way of expressing and bringing out the deeper meanings of words to inspire and motivate others.

Vulnerability is a sensitive but important subject because it can be so powerful. When it is met with intention and courage, it can lead to a transformation and a sense of oneness with others, and as such, results will yield (V.I.C.T.O.R.Y.). As we grow, we also feel a sense of oneness and alignment with something powerful, so much so that we begin to live it (G.O.A.L.).

After all, we are aiming for results that we envision which are worthy of us and we ourselves as worthy of them. Therefore, we take action because we have a reason that drives us (R.E.W.A.R.D.).

Regardless of where you start, it is important to have posture. One of the best definitions for posture (which I have heard from a mentor) is the belief in what you have regardless of external acceptance, approval, or agreement. Another interpretation of mine is the basic understanding that success involves a network and evolves around service and significance (B.U.S.I.N.E.S.S.). A notable point about great leaders is people are inspired by and want to follow them. I once heard a quote from a mentor years ago that stated, "Managers inherit subordinates. Leaders earn followers."

I recently heard another mentor mention that people want to know they can belong with you, that you love them, and that they can trust you. (B.L.T.)

At some point in business and life, you will run into situations and failures (yes, I said it—failures) that will test you and continue to do so. How you deal with these situations will define you, but most importantly, you must grow and become a better person from them.

I have had my share of personal issues and failure in life and business, many of which compelled and inspired me to write this content. I'm a firm believer that what you go through in life builds your character, and as such, four years of alcohol abuse from 2009 to 2013 that sprung from personal issues and events that followed, including my father passing away, made me a stronger person. This experience taught me a lot about mindset and the importance of sobriety and clarity of mind. I am always learning and growing like we all need to if we are to create a beautiful lifestyle inspired by service and significance (B.L.I.S.S.). Exactly what this is will be mostly different depending on our purpose and desires—essentially what drives us.

Having a belief that I am blessed with much love and peace gives me the strength to have the courage of my convictions. At the same time, I'm empowered by faith and grace to have gratitude for the service I give and the abundance that I receive. It is something I am constantly affirming to the infinite spirit (I.S.) referred to as the subconscious by another mentor.

Through my learnings, I have come to understand that success is something that you achieve. Its significance, though also important for oneself, is what you give to others that propels them forward. This requires courage of your convictions, which I believe leads to confidence and a level of certainty where you can connect to the source (higher power). If you do not have the first four, then I believe there is an inner conflict that needs resolving to move forward.

A method I have created to calm and relax myself and move on from experiences that are not serving is the following: Bless and release an emotion, event, or person; envision what you want to attract in that present moment; become aware of this; and know it as your truth. Honour yourself and others in that moment by being your higher self and embracing the energy that comes with this (B.R.E.A.T.H.E.). I delve into this to remind you to let it go of anything at that moment that's not serving you, and again honour yourself and others by being your higher self, and let this be your truth (L.I.G.H.T.). Breathe light into a situation, so to speak.

All these acronyms, thoughts, and quotes I have written here are meant to express my way of thinking, show you what I have learnt, and give you a broader perspective on leadership and matters relating to this subject. I hope you will revisit this and reflect on it time and again when you desire to do so.

Being an effective leader requires all the qualities written here, and I am sure that you can name many others you've thought of and learnt through various thought leaders. Leading by example is probably one of the most important qualities.

The gift to envision new intelligence that uplifts the spirit (G.E.N.I.U.S.) is another great quality of a leader who is always innovating and searching for new ways to build teams and organisations. People with character, heart, authenticity, charm, integrity, and optimism are candidates for great leaders. As I have mentioned earlier, the ability to find the leader within makes us lead others.

A great leader is also an excellent promoter. They have a purpose behind getting their resources out to the masses, the outcome for which is to transfer value and enhance lives

(P.R.O.M.O.T.E.). This takes courage of conviction, confidence, and ruthlessness of action to create momentum.

Results are the ultimate truth, so when you hustle, you can be limitless while embracing service and significance (R.U.T.H.L.E.S.S.). That is the positive expansion of the word ruthless. Be ruthless when required, and then understand that love is the end game, so to speak, and that the state you're in is most important (R.U.L.E.S.). By this, I am referring to emotional state, or peak state, and even beautiful state of mind, which you may have heard certain mentors and public figures mention.

For this, I am practicing what I refer to as transition intention, meaning that when I transition from one task to another, I ask myself, "What is my upcoming intention?" and to practice it while in a peak state to achieve results (T.I.P.A.R.). I came up with this method after observing certain leaders attain great results.

Great leaders are professionals, and as such, they get results that are ongoing with grace on their side, being ruthless as described, while embracing self-love and being focused on a peak/beautiful state (P.R.O.G.R.E.S.S.).

Time and again, I have heard the word "value" because the more of it you add to people's lives, the more you receive in return. Hence, the more you ask, "How can I add value?" the more you have value.

As leaders, especially when we are presenting or building a team or an organisation, we are presenting a lifestyle opportunity for those who see the vision and embrace it (L.O.V.E.). That's how you bring passionate people together.

Another important factor in leading is being sincere in your efforts to lead someone to a lifestyle change, have integrity in doing so, and network with grace (S.E.L.L.I.N.G.) No matter what a great leader sells, they do it with those qualities.

You may have heard the word "alpha," which refers to a confident person who shows up with much love and in an empowered state. It is also ruthless as my definition, and this is their truth (A.L.E.R.T.). These people just embrace and do it! (J.E.D.I.).

The most important feature of a leader is the alignment of the spiritual, emotional, mental, and physical aspects of their lifestyle in order to build an empire (S.E.M.P.L.E.). On a final note, leaders are enthusiastic as they network and give value to attract their tribe. With grace, they build an empire (E.N.G.A.G.E.). Once again, my purpose for this material is to provide you with an alternate view of leadership and use this as a reference guide to make your mark as a leader.

BIOGRAPHY

Shane Adams is a network marketer developing next-level leaders by inspiring people with what he has learned and experienced from some of the best leaders in the industry. He is a member of leadership development groups and regularly speaks online about the importance of personal development in becoming an effective leader. He aims to help people live life on their terms by working with his organisation and assisting people through lifestyle coaching with the brand "Master your Mind, Wealth and Wellness."

Connect with Shane Adams via https://linktr.ee/ShaneAdams

CHAPTER 29

IT BEGINS WITH A DECISION

By Shantal Wallace

I looked in the pantry and stared at the tin of baked beans and a half-empty packet of rice. Aside from other condiments and a head of lettuce that had seen better days, I thought, 'What could I make for dinner with this?' This was a fairly common scenario in my home those days when no one else was around to witness the lengths I went to just to make ends meet. I did this to save every spare dollar I had in the bank to provide whatever was needed for my nine-year-old son.

When he was home with me, I ensured he had everything he needed. But I wanted to give him more than just the bare necessities. You see, I had a very privileged childhood. I had more toys than any child should ever have, and I had traveled across four continents with my parents by the time I was ten years old. My boy was only a year younger than I was back then, and I couldn't offer him those same privileges. In fact, I thought I'd never have the financial capability to give him the kind of life he deserved. It was a highly depressive thought and one that I regularly repeated to myself: 'You'll never have more money.'

At the time, I also didn't know that by telling myself I would never have more, I was limiting myself in every aspect of my life and living with a poverty mindset. I was stressed and anxious every day and sometimes cried for no reason at all. When my son wasn't home with me, I would drink and wallow in self-pity—something I haven't spoken about to anyone but my closest friends. I was ashamed to admit this. Severe depression had set in, but I had no idea at that stage. Through constant psychological turmoil, I ended up developing weight and diet issues, social anxiety, and a stress-related outbreak of severe Dyshidrotic Eczema. If you don't know what that is, it's a fairly common non-contagious skin disorder or irritation where tiny fluid-filled blisters develop on your skin, usually on the hands, fingers, or feet. The blisters cause an immense itching sensation, and I've practically mutated my fingers and hands as a result of scratching. When it's really bad, the affected areas of my left hand (which seems to be the area most regularly impacted) become very dry and cracked, sometimes splitting the skin open. It becomes very painful at that stage.

Rewind to 2016. It was a few months prior to my marriage coming to an abrupt end. I had been married to my high school sweetheart for seven years, and we had just moved from the capital city of Brisbane back to the regional city of Rockhampton. That's actually where we met when my parents, sister, and I had moved over from New Zealand in 2001. I was born in South Africa, and we immigrated to New Zealand when I was eleven years old. So, this had been the second culture and climate shock for me.

When my then-husband and I decided to move back to Rockhampton in June 2015, we did it to be closer to the family after having our beautiful baby boy. The only problem was that I couldn't secure a job in my field despite having applied for jobs three months before moving. I worked in human resources for twelve years and had a wide background across several industries, yet no one offered me an interview.

To ensure I had some form of income, my parents offered me a contract job at my father's business as they didn't have access to a human resources expert. They often called me for advice in the past. So, I worked in our family business part-time while continuing to look for work. It was incredibly generous of them to allow me the opportunity. However, it wasn't the right fit for me, so I knew it would only be temporary.

I soon realized I couldn't keep using the same traditional approach to secure work. I was applying for jobs online, which wasn't that often due to the limited HR roles in the local area. At the first sight of a new role, I went straight into it. I simply wasn't getting any response, though. This went on for more than a year. So, I decided to hire out my services and expertise to small businesses in the local and surrounding areas so that I could keep doing what I loved.

And so, I established my own business as a sole trader, and over the three and a half years I ran my consulting business, I had quite a few good clients. However, this wasn't enough to be financially sustainable. I had made the mistake of investing in every tool, software program, marketing avenue, and online training to become a successful entrepreneur. Not to mention the business tax I had to pay. I was in serious debt, and it was just getting worse!

When my husband and I no longer saw a healthy future together, not only was I in serious debt, the work that I was carrying out required me to travel, and I made myself available 24/7. I was literally hustling like a cash-crazy pimp! How on earth was I going to get myself out of debt if I wasn't able to work even harder and longer hours to generate more income? How was I going to care for my son under those circumstances? What kind of life was this?

I started to spiral into self-pity and told myself that I was a complete failure. My marriage had failed. I failed to create financial security and a healthy environment for my son, and I hated having to say, 'No, mummy can't afford that on a regular basis.' I was gaining weight and hardly getting any sleep with my mind working overtime . . . and without any real focus.

Now, my son doesn't ask for much. In fact, he's kind of like an old soul and has the kindest heart you can imagine. Whenever I'd say things like, 'I'm sorry that I can't give you more right now, Robbie,' he would say, 'Mum! You give me more than I could ever ask for. You're the best mum in the whole world!' I would, of course, get teary and express my endless and unconditional love and gratitude for having this amazing blessing in my life. He gave me the will to carry on and try harder every single day. He's the reason I'm still around to tell my story today.

You see, I was brought up with the mantra, "To strive for excellence and nothing less was acceptable." From a young age, I was the top student in my class in several disciplines, particularly mathematics, drama, and sports. I was so determined to be the best at everything, and at times, I did so at the cost of others. I was still young and had many hard life lessons to learn. When I felt I hadn't achieved the absolute best, I really struggled to deal with the feeling of failure. I'm still highly self-critical of my own efforts and achievements, but I am on my own personal mindset journey to help turn this energy into something positive and motivating.

Back to my schooling years and how the thought of failure almost debilitated me at times, I remember taking a maths test one day (I was nine years old at the time). I was looking at the final grade I had received, marked in the iconic red correction pen that our educators (teachers) loved so dearly. Within moments, I couldn't see her handwriting on the page anymore because my eyes had welled up with giant-sized tears at the result. Thirty-eight out of forty. THIRTY-EIGHT OUT OF FORTY! That was 95 percent, by the way. I was shattered. I hadn't achieved 100 percent. What would my parents think of me? What would they say?!

As it stands, they were happy with my result and surprised that I had gotten so upset about my marks. This demonstrates the type of pressure and expectation I placed upon myself from a young age, having developed the perception that nothing less than excellence was acceptable. Good enough simply wouldn't do either. This 'story' that I've been telling myself for my entire life has been both my superpower and my kryptonite.

It has been my superpower for the reason that I always pushed myself to achieve the highest standard or possible outcome of anything and everything I chose to commit myself to. I simply had to be the best at everything. If I wasn't, it just wasn't good enough. It's the reason why I've always put my career first, and I would go to extreme lengths to prove my worth to my employers. Despite my work ethic and putting in way too many hours than anyone ever should, especially when they have a family at home, I felt like I was hardly making any progress throughout my fifteen years in the corporate world. It felt like a lifelong battle just to get a pay raise or promotion to the next rung in the ladder. It was exhausting putting so much in and getting so little out of it.

In April 2019, after having applied for what seemed to be hundreds of HR jobs, still relying on working part-time for my family business in a role that wasn't suited to me and having landed in more debt than I knew what to do with, I decided to completely give up on HR. I knew what my skills were and what motivated me, so I looked into becoming a qualified wedding and event planner. I wanted to do something fun with my talent and skills. I had been worn out and burnt out for too long, and it was time for a change.

I started an online course in June 2019, and I accepted that this meant no longer looking to climb the next rung on the ladder in the corporate HR world. Having had my heart set on becoming a director or head of human resources before I turned forty took a massive hit on my career aspirations; it was a tough blow to my ego. I didn't really have a goal anymore when I gave up my career and just thought about how much I needed a change.

I ended up securing a job in July 2019 as a receptionist/ waitress at a local resort, and I applied for government assistance to ensure I could financially meet my obligations as a parent regarding school fees, maintenance costs, etc. I needed to provide everything my child needed, no matter what. So, my next chapter began with a minimum wage, study, and cutting any unnecessary costs from our lives.

I received a surprise phone call only a month later and secured a job back in the HR corporate world. I jumped at the opportunity because I knew it would give me financial security. What it led to, though, was a full realization that, once again, I was placing myself in an environment and circumstances where I would continue to be limited in my personal, professional, and financial goals. I was still scraping through from week to week, and I knew deep inside, there must be another way.

So, I made a life-changing decision. The kind of decision that would place me on a path very different from what I had previously walked. Different from what I had previously believed about what I was worth, what I could achieve, and what was possible. I took a leap of faith based on massive-determined action because I knew it was the only way to create the life I wanted for my son and me. As Pablo Picasso puts it beautifully, "Action is the foundational key to all success."[13]

---

13 "Pablo Picasso Quotes," BrainyQuote (Xplore), accessed October 11, 2021, https://www.brainyquote.com/quotes/pablo_picasso_120309.

BIOGRAPHY

Residing in Rockhampton, Australia, Shantal Wallace has always strived for excellence in every endeavour. With a bachelor's degree in human resources management, a graduate certificate in management, coupled with over fifteen years working with business leaders and small business owners, she dedicates her talent and skills to seeing others succeed, personally and professionally. Having faced many trials and tribulations throughout her life, Shantal is a solo mum and entrepreneur who is passionate about making her mark in the world. Her mission as a global online business coach is to help those who are seeking change in making the shift from employee to entrepreneur. With leadership influences such as Simon Sinek, Tony Robbins, Margie Warrell, and Oprah Winfrey, Shantal believes that everyone deserves a life of greatness, and that transformation begins with a decision.

Connect with Shantal Wallace via https://linktr.ee/ShantalWallace

CHAPTER 30

THE WEIGHT OF YOUR EXCUSES

By Tracy Laughard

I stared at the credit card swiper. There it was again.

DECLINED!

That stupid word seemed to haunt me everywhere I went. I fumbled through my handful of credit cards, all of which were maxed out, in order to find the money to pay for my daughter's pull-ups.

Unable to find a card that would work and embarrassed as all hell, I took the pull-ups back to the shelf, silently walked out to my car, feeling as if every eye in the store was on me, sat in the driver seat, and I cried.

See, I thought I had done all the right things. I graduated high school at the top of my class, went to a university on a scholarship and got my teaching degree, went on to get my master's in mental health counseling, and graduated and got a school counseling job right out of graduate school. On top of that, I was a great counselor and a great teacher.

Yet, I just had to put away pull-ups for my daughter because I had chosen to pay our past-due light bill earlier that day.

So, what happened between that day and today? Because today looks very different for me. Now, I'm a six-figure earner, a top leader in network marketing, and speaking on stage at events. I get to travel to many places, and I run my business full-time from home around my kid's schedules. I'm my own boss, and I own my time.

What changed was that I realized just how heavy my excuses really were. And if I was going to really fly like I was meant to, I was going to have to drop them. So, I did.

I was a very green network marketer at this moment, crying in my car at a Dollar Store parking lot. I had just joined my friend and saw the potential with this industry and said, "I am going all-in with this! I'm gonna be a top earner and quit my job so I can get that time freedom and financial freedom I very much want."

But when it came down to it, I had every excuse in the book for why I couldn't show up consistently for my business.

But what I realized at that moment, while I was crying in my car, embarrassed and stressed the hell out, was that my excuses for not doing what I needed to do to grow my business were keeping me stuck exactly where I was.

Every single network marketer, every single entrepreneur, has had that come-to-Jesus moment where they had to get real with themselves about their excuses.

Maybe you're in that moment right now.

We use excuses for why we "can't" do the things we know we need to do to turn it around in our businesses.

So many in this industry wonder why they're not moving forward. But what I have found is that the growth of your business typically boils down to your consistency and intentionality.

Sure, I was broke as broke could be. I had no time, no money, and took care of two autistic kids who needed my time and financial support to get them the services they needed. I felt very low at that moment.

I got real with myself instead of continuing to play the victim and say, "I can't because . . ."

I COULD. I was just making excuses not to.

When teammates or the people I coach come to me and say they just can't seem to move forward in their business, I ask them the same questions I asked myself in the parking lot that day: What actions did you take today to move the needle forward in your business?

And usually, the answer I get is a whole lot of EXCUSES. Well, I haven't had time. My job got in the way. My kids. Traveling. I don't have the online following I need. I'm not as pretty as her. I can't take social media pictures like her. I can't get on video because of my kids. Old Aunt Suzy's cousin had a cookout we had to go to instead. I can't . . . I can't . . . I can't . . . . And the list goes on.

I had a lot of the same reasons why I "couldn't."

But let's label them what they were because they certainly weren't reasons. They were ALL excuses.

The key to you moving the needle forward in your business is for you to DROP the excuses.

Your goal, dream, vision—you—deserve all the wins. You owe it to yourself to drop your excuses and do what you need to do to build your legacy business.

Now here's what I want you to do to change it. And it's exactly what I did that day in my car. Every time you have an excuse, I want you to rephrase it. Instead of saying you can't do something you know you need to do for your business, I want you to change the words to, "It's not a priority," and then see how that feels. It's important to switch the language because it forces you to take ownership of it.

When you use excuses, you're essentially pointing the blame elsewhere. It then gets out of your control, and you turn yourself into a victim of your circumstances.

You're blaming your kids, your husband, your job, your dog, or Aunt Suzy for the fact that you can't grow in your business. But what it really boils down to is you and your consistency and intentionality in your business.

So, when you switch the language, you take ownership of your actions and what you choose to do. Then, you can CHANGE it! Which is a damn beautiful thing, friends!

Instead of saying, "I don't have time for my business because of Aunt Suzy's cookout," I want you to change the words to "My business is not a priority. Aunt Suzy's cookout is."

How does that taste? Is it a little salty?

If it doesn't bother you one bit, then no worries! If that sits well with your soul, that's absolutely fine. But if it's a little salty, and you WANT your business to be a priority because your why and your vision for your life and your family's life is a priority, then you can start taking the action you've been avoiding on the top of your to-do list for that day.

The simple trick of switching the language is going to allow you to check what's really a priority for you. Because if your excuses are stronger than your vision, and your why and your business aren't a priority, that's okay! This isn't always going to be a priority for every person. But you can't be upset when you're not rakin' in the six-to-seven figures, and you're not hitting top ranks in your company. For your business to pay you like a business, you have to treat it like a business, which means it HAS to be a priority.

When I changed the language for myself, it tasted pretty salty to me, and I decided that day that my excuses were no longer going to stop me. So, I dropped them. And that's a good thing! The best thing about this is you can drop the excuses anytime.

The biggest excuse I used was time. I would tell myself I had no time to build my business. Now granted, my schedule was pretty jam-packed, but the bottom line was I DID have time. We all have the same twenty-four hours in a day. People who were busier than me were making the time, so I just had to do the same thing and quit with the excuses. My excuse for not being consistent with my business was that I had no time, but I NEEDED more time.

If you are in network marketing, you have time freedom in the palm of your hands. As a network marketer, you can create all the time freedom you want! But I was too busy using it as my excuse. But the bottom line is we MAKE time for our priorities. Once I changed the language from "I can't because . . ." to "It's not a priority," well, that stung a little. So, I let that excuse go and made my business a priority by showing up daily, consistently. I got up earlier before work to build my business. I used my lunch hour. After I put my kids to bed at night, I stayed up and built my business. And eventually, I was able to quit my full-time teaching job because my business had replaced that income.

There could be a number of things holding you back in your business. Maybe it's making that first post on social media about your business. Maybe it's getting on video and going live about your opportunity or talking to that one person that you know would crush it and you would love to work with, but you're afraid of what they might think. Maybe it's not showing up to coaching calls with your mentor and being coachable. Whatever it is that is stopping you, switch the language and instead say, "This is not a priority."

Before that moment in the car where I essentially had to choose between the light bill and my daughter's pull-ups, my business wasn't truly a priority for me. I liked to say it was, but my actions spoke much louder than my words because I wasn't actually taking action to grow my business. And those excuses were really coming from fear.

I was afraid I would fall flat on my face.

I was an educated person. What would my peers say?

I was afraid of judgment.

I was afraid I would be throwing away money and time on something that was a "scam."

I was afraid of what people would say when I reached out to them.

I was afraid of rejection.

And out of that fear, I would come up with excuses.

I don't have time.

I don't have money.

I can't because . . . .

But isn't that the point of this industry, though? To GAIN more time freedom? More financial freedom?

It was definitely my why for getting started in this industry. I needed more time freedom. I needed more financial freedom. I needed to be able to BREATHE instead of feeling trapped in these time and money constraints. Yet, here I was, using my exact why as my excuse.

Friends, your why can NEVER be your excuse. Y'all know I've never been known for sugar coating things. But I'm telling this story because I LOVE YOU. I don't care if I've never met you before in my life, I LOVE YOU, and you deserve the life you want. And THIS MOMENT was the exact moment when I decided that my excuses were no longer going to be the thing that held me back from my potential any longer. My excuses were no longer going to keep me stuck in this place where I had to choose between a light bill and pull-ups. My excuses were no longer going to keep me from creating the dream and vision I had for myself and my family. And my excuses were no longer going to stop me from building a legacy that would not only impact my family but would allow me to pour into other people who were in the same situation and empower them to take action to get themselves MOVING.

I want you to start being self-aware. I want you to think of what is stopping you from getting to that next level in your business, and I want you to switch the language. Is it an excuse, or is it just not a priority? And if it is a priority, then TAKE THE ACTION and do it. Do it scared. Do it imperfectly. Just take the messy, imperfect action because that is what is going to get you to that next level. The messy, imperfect action is what took me from crying in my car, unable to buy pull-ups for my daughter to become a six-figure earner, earning seven figures in team sales, speaking on stage at company events, having a following of tens of thousands, and having the ability to speak life into YOU through this book.

Drop the excuses, friend. Take the messy action. DO THE DO. Get out of your comfort zone, and make it happen. Because you can, and you will.

BIOGRAPHY

Tracy Laughard is a former teacher-turned-CEO and has been a network marketer for four years. She is a top recruiter, top leader, has generated well over seven figures in team sales, and has spoken on stage at company events. She is also a social media marketing coach and mentor, helping network marketers build their businesses on social media through influencer marketing. She is the host of the 5-Star rated podcast "That Social Marketing Chick" and has been featured in Business For Home. Her favorite titles are "Mom" and "Wife." She married her high school sweetheart, has two kids, is an avid road-tripper, and a self-proclaimed potato chip addict.

Connect with Tracy Laughard via https://linktr.ee/tracylaughard

CHAPTER 31

THE JOURNEY TO FREEDOM

By Will Hartford

At first, I did not understand the corporate lie. I was always told: "If you do a good job and listen to your boss, you can advance." It was my first corporate job, albeit it was a small company. Due to my interaction issues, I tried to get into the testing department several times because this would keep my work in flux, and I would not get bored. I was turned down many times, but eventually, I got into one of the advanced groups, which had a cool personal milestone that I would not figure out until a few years later. I inadvertently had a hand in creating Blu-Ray technology because they were using our hardware to test with and would call our support line.

Fast forward a little, and I was still craving a challenge from my job. My older friends landed IT jobs with our local college, and I talked to them about getting a campus job. Even though I knew more than most applicants with my experience level, I was told I needed a degree. Many of the jobs offered a deal that if you finished at least two years, then you could get hired and finish your schooling while you worked. This sounded great. Only one problem: I could not afford to go to my local school. I ended up going to a tech school in the metro. While attending school, I found that I needed more time to do my homework, and my current job was not playing nice since I was in school, even though the employee handbook stated that if you had an early class, you'd still get your hours. Plus, due to an upcoming change in the next big operating system and other hardware improvements in other companies, the rumor going around was they would cut back on employees if our support volume went down. It actually did, and two years later, they closed that support center.

I ended up getting a tech support job with a major corporation thinking that would be better as the company was stable. However, once again, I saw the lie. After working there for a short time, I discovered a solution to an issue that would help save money and make more profit. The downside was that the client would pay less money upfront but would save money and make us a higher profit due to not having to send out as many field techs. In short, I was told my idea was stupid because it would affect the overall cash flow. Even though the company could ultimately make more money and save their customers' money as well, this was wrong. Even though in my mind, I knew I was right, I knew this was a major corporation, and they worked on cash flow. At the end of the day, they get the profits based on the write-offs they generate against the company revenue. The other frustrating thing was when I graduated with my Associate's Computer Science Degree, I did not get any credit for it at work. And a few years later, the US Board of Education shut the school and several others down. Depending on who looks at it, they do not take it seriously. I pretty much wasted my time and money.

Then, one day, I was talking to one of my best friends, and we started to talk about starting our own business. See, when I was out of high school, one of my older friends ran a local hobby shop, and I would do tasks for him for credit. I enjoyed doing it because this was my other love—being a computer, console, and paper gamer. This sparked my interest because if I worked a job I loved, then I could not go wrong. He also knew I had tried to start my own computer store servicing the rural folks in the area on-site. But my partner kind of dropped off the radar and did not have time to keep it going while I was in school for the little bit of profit I got out of it. He also knew I was repairing gaming consoles. He figured that we would start there and then get into renting system time like the person he used to work for did. We started, and I took a queue from one of my other friends, a VP for a restaurant chain, and put his extra money into the store. I did the same with my extra pay. The only issue with the job I had was that they had strict rules on what I could and could not do. I could be the owner but not the CEO/President. I wrote a contract with my friend to take on the role while I had my job. We did great and even upgraded to a bigger location at one point and even a second store.

Like a lot of things in my life, it goes back to my upbringing. One thing that comes up is that I am a preacher's kid. Now I know what a lot of you are thinking: "Were not these the ones who got in trouble all the time?" Well, in my case, this was not true. In fact, I actually had a conversation with my parents. They were frustrated due to the fact that they raised me right, because of which I have trouble being a "good businessman." I am not ruthless or hard enough with the people under me. Also, in college, my nickname was the "Diet Coke of Evil" because I was so nice to people. Even when I was in any role play or theatre group, I would have trouble playing any kind of evil character. I would even have friends tell me I need to be more assertive, stand up for myself, and say no when I did not agree with something.

This is where many of my troubles began because, at the time, I got everything I needed, so my personal expenses went down, and all I would need to do is pay for my personal bills since the stores were paying for themselves. I got a remote contact job to cover my bills. That created some problems because I did not have any emergency/rainy day funds to take care of any mishaps that might come up. Little did I know that my friend had been slowly upsetting and losing customers while I had not been in the store, and he even upset the store manager. He was one of the reasons why people only came in to window shop and hang out with him rather than spend money. I tried to address the issue, but he pretty much gave me the attitude claiming that I stood up to everyone but him. We also had a board of members, many of whom he had turn against me. Today, most of them have apologized to me. They said I was right and should have listened. So, I was down and out with nothing to show during this time, but I did learn something important. I know this can be done with the right people and the right tools.

This is something you will pick up in the business world. Most successful people are asked: What would you do if you lost everything today? Most of them already know the exact plan they would take to get back what they had, and the important part of this would be that, in most cases, they would be able to do it better and usually faster as they would know what worked and what did not. With that in mind, enter another one of my friends for whom I was working part-time. This was because, at the time, we did not know the direction low voltage was going. So, I was working on my electrical license to connect these mixed devices and power myself. He said he saw what happened with my other friend and me. Little did I know at the time, he was playing both sides of the fence to help himself. We tried to restart the business again, but this time, with the knowledge that I had. Also, due to the allegation of my former business partner, I would not have direct access to the store money other than with the customer-facing side. I agreed, just to show that my knowledge and experience were on point. Since I fostered the relationship with my suppliers and knew where the best prices were, and they would deal with all the backend, I would still get paid for what I loved to do . . . while I repaired my name. I bought into this because he was an aspiring politician and had all the ability to tell you what you wanted to hear. I did not catch on until one day he was talking to a mutual friend in the other room, and I could hear him trying to flip the conversation to his favor. After this, I started to call him out on our conversations when he tried that on me. At one point, he stated that we did not have the money to order products for the store, and I told him my account had profits in it. Then, I saw the same lie that the big corporation used on me because a few days before, he was joking with me he had made 10,000 in sales, and I made 1,000 on my side. At this point, I asked him what his profit was. He said it was one percent, whereas mine was around thirty-five percent after expenses. I told him that if I had more products, I could have had more sales. Since those were my own sales accounts, I asked him if I could order the product that we needed, and I would pay the expenses and keep the profits to prove to him this works. I thought he'd agree because he thought I was going to fail. However, I knew my products and when I needed to have them. I made 3,000 in profit in one weekend. This was the start of the downfall. I tried to get him in so we could go over things, but he kept blowing me off. In the end, we lost an account because he tried to get rid of me.

While this was going on, several of my close friends saw me do this in the midst of all my problems, and they started talking to me about running a store for them. However, the money and timing were bad for both. Then, enter another friend I had back in school, and they were talking about wanting to open a store, asking for my help. After talking a bit about it, I agreed to bring my resources to help them get started and planned to stay connected for at least two years to help get them started. I also added that if they wanted to do their own thing, I would cut them loose and pull back my investment funds. Once again, little did I know that they were screwing me by making back deals behind my back. So, fast forward a year later, they pretty much ended up stabbing me in the back. I did get some justice in the end because they lost the business.

I am not the type of person who gives up either, so I gave it another shot and made it work for two years, even to the point where I was sleeping in my office and taking showers at my friend's place nearby. Unfortunately, all the negative talk pretty much affected things to the point that I was not getting the customers I was used to. At this time, I started to get back to online sales and realized that if I kept burning the candle all over, I would not even have one left for myself. So, I decided to put the retail store on hold and focus on getting resources. Enter my primary mentor. He helped put me back on the track I needed to be to get things back to where I wanted them. I also knew this would not happen overnight. I noticed part of my problem was that I jumped too fast without having everything properly in place. The first main thing that he stated was, "You need to look at your expenses and make sure you have thrice that amount before you quit your traditional job." At that moment, the light shone on the main mistake I kept making. The next thing that happened was that the techy in me started to help people, and I found that I enjoyed getting people through tech hurdles and helping them find the right offers to succeed. As they succeeded, so did I because it took me back to one of my loves: Tech. Then, over time, I would get more freedom to do the things that I enjoyed and loved.

As I keep walking this journey, I find myself going back to my original roots, finding tools and information that work well together, and sharing them for the betterment of all. Now, at this point, I am on the road to fully having my freedom realized. Yes, there are negative people and naysayers in your life, but none of them matter. Eject them from your reality and never give up on your dreams because only you have the plans and resources in place for you to do the things you want.

BIOGRAPHY

Will Hartford is the owner of Cloud Consortium, a company helping business owners find the tools to help them implement scaling their business. He is an experienced marketer with several programs and software under his belt. This enables him to find the one that best meets one's business needs. In addition, he is an experienced technical writer, having worked for companies like Creative Labs and Dell, writing training and instruction sets.

Connect with Will Hartford via https://linktr.ee/issken

THE END